TODDLERS ARE A**HOLES
(IT'S NOT YOUR FAULT)

SOPHA KING TYERD

ISBN: 978-0-9905928-9-1

DISCLAIMER

This book is self-published. No fancy publishing house. No high-paid editors. No team of marketing people wearing real clothes. Just me in my $9 yoga pants, sitting in a toy-and-balled-up-pee-pee-diaper-covered living room with Caillou's Apprentice next to me, begging for snacks and dumping out my purse. If an occasional typo bothers you terribly, feel free to hire me a nanny and I'll get them taken care of in the next book.

—SFT

Dear Reader,

I'm assuming that you're reading this book because you have a toddler. First, I'm sorry. Second, don't show any weakness. Toddlers, like all animals of prey, feed off of fear.

"Toddler Assholery" is a normal part of human development. It's like puberty but focuses mainly on throwing food on the floor and taking swings at people who pay your way in life.

Reader, never ever blame yourself for your toddler being an asshole to you. Toddlers are beautiful, kind, and wonderful to people who are not in primary custody of them.

There's a reason toddlers are at their peak cuteness: it's because nature knows that toddlerhood is when you are most likely to take your child to a public park and leave them there with a note that says, "I'm a little shit and they couldn't take it anymore."

If you are lying in bed with a glass of wine, your house destroyed by a 20lb Tasmanian devil, please know that you're not alone. Toddlers are assholes. They just are. Remind yourself of this fact the next time your 2-year old is screaming like her hair is on fire in the Ikea parking lot or your 18-month old tosses a full bowl of oatmeal across the room. The oatmeal he cried for. The oatmeal you dragged your sleep-deprived ass out of bed at 4:45AM to make.

Remind yourself of this when you're about to judge your stay-at-home spouse for the condition the home is in, or that fact that he or she is still in their pajamas at dinner. They've been under house arrest with a little asshole all day. Chill. It wouldn't kill you to bring home dinner and rum, either.

When you feel tempted to ask your friend with a 3-year old why they don't call you or hang out anymore, remember that they're being kept hostage. Send them an Edible Arrangements or better yet, offer to babysit for free while they roam Target eating popcorn and sipping on a Frappuccino for several hours.

I hope you enjoy this book. Go fill up your wine. You deserve it.

Kindly,
Sopha King Tyerd

This book is dedicated to my adorable assholes. Despite making my hair fall out, I think we have a good thing going

TABLE OF CONTENTS

TODDLERS ARE A**HOLES

CHAPTER 1
WHAT IS A TODDLER?

A toddler is a cross between a sociopath, rabid animal, cocker spaniel, demon and an angel. Depending on the time of day and when their last meal was, you will see all aspects of your toddler's persona. Below is an average toddler's schedule:

3AM – Wake up with a cry so loud that it will send a rush of adrenaline through your parent's body and destroy your their hope of ever feeling rested.

3:01AM – Demand breakfast at decibel levels only heard at raves and political protests

3:03AM – Eat a NutriGrain bar on the living room floor while your parent sits slumped over on the couch.

3:05AM – Cry for no reason and demand channel changes.

3:07AM – Crumble NutriGrain bar in your hand and smash it into your hair.

3:15AM – Watch cartoons with a sleeve of Ritz crackers that your parents threw at you in desperation.

4AM – Pee on the floor.

5AM – Cry in your parent's ear while jumping on their genitals.

7AM – Snack time. Eat almost none of it.

8AM – Nap because yes, you woke up that fucking early.

9AM – More TV because your parent can't deal with you.

10AM to 5PM – Destroy the house or daycare. Make it look like a FEMA-neglected natural disaster. Nap here and there.

5PM – Get thrown at whichever parent who is having the most manageable panic attack.

6PM – Ruin dinner for everyone.

7PM – Go batshit crazy about bath/brushing teeth/pajamas. It's important to act like this is you first time every going through the bedtime routine.

9PM – Pass out.

To a person like Nanny Jo of Supernanny or a sanctimonious parent, this will look insane. Regular parents of toddlers recognize this as their life.

Note to sanctiparents: Shut the fuck up. Nobody wants to hear your strategies for dealing with your perfect $300 European designer tunic wearing children who shit rainbows and gold coins, or about your amazing disciplinary techniques, or your Instagram-ready meals of figs, brown rice bread and homemade goat cheese from your free-range talking backyard goats. If you humble brag about how your toddler has been sleeping through the night since he was four minutes old we're going to pull that stick out of your ass and beat you with it. Go ahead and keep pretending on Facebook that you're a perfect parent but remember, some of us know you in real life.

Like serial killers, toddlers struggle with empathy. When your toddler wakes you up with a kick to the head realize it's not because they hate you, but because they view you as a slave. You see, toddlers are primarily concerned with meeting their own needs and do not recognize that you too are a human person. To a toddler, you do not have a heart, mind, or soul, you are simply a skin-covered robot tall enough to reach the candy on top of the fridge. You are an epidermis bag and source of endless comfort. Don't take toddler behavior personally because it isn't about you.

How do I deal with my toddler's behavior?

Do what most parents do and drown your frustrations in doughnuts and beer come bedtime. Personal trainers and fitness nuts will tell you that eating before bed is bad for your health and waistline but what these idiots don't understand is that you need to snack so that you don't abandon your family in the night.

When it comes down to it, isn't it preferable to inhale a bag of Doritos and be 40-50lbs overweight than to leave your toddler without a parent? Obviously, you're doing the right thing by eating your emotions.

Consider the below an official prescription for numbing the pain of living with a toddler human:

LATE NIGHT FOOD PRESCRIPTION:
(bring this to any convenience store)

Name: _____ (write your name)

Medicine:

- Homemade nachos

- Midnight Bagel and Cream Cheese

- Fruit Cup (just kidding, this one is a joke. Fruit can't solve problems.)

- Bag of Skittles

- Snickers Bars

- Unlimited Popcorn

- Cookies

- Ice Cream

- Frozen appetizers like potato skins with cheddar cheese and bacon

- Wine

- Rum

- Any liquor

- Beer

No one is going to judge you for shame-eating Peeps in December to get through potty training. Everybody does it. Get fancy and try out some crazy recipes. Ideas below.

- Dessert Nachos. Make these with Cinnamon Toast Crunch, melted butter, and crushed up Pop Tarts.

- Green Smoothies. Blend up vodka and mint chip ice-cream. Bam. There's calcium in there, too. Calcium for your bones.

- Toddler Snack Trail Mix. Take revenge on your small child by mixing all of their favorite snacks in a large bowl. Throw in their Goldfish crackers, yogurt-covered raisins, cereal, and whatever else you can find. Eat this by the greedy ass handful while watching Wipeout.

- Salad. In a bowl mix together chopped bacon, chopped boiled eggs, and lots of mayonnaise. Eat it at 2AM while crying.

- Living with a toddler isn't the time for you to be worried about having a thigh gap. Fun fact: You can actually create a thigh gap no matter what you weight by just standing with your legs apart. See? Gap.

It's possible that you can get so depressed from living with a toddler that you may need prescription medication from an actual doctor in the form of antidepressants. I'm telling you, having a toddler is no fucking joke. In that case, be sure to jot down whatever you're taking and the dosage in your child's baby book. When they look back on their milestones they'll also see the damage they did to your mental health. Hopefully this will inspire them to major in something serious like biology or political science rather than ceramics so that they'll make money and take care of you the way you deserve. No one ever made millions hand crafting clay pots.

There is no shame in being medicated. Like I said, at least you're still there. Anything you can do to keep from packing up your shit and leaving.

What Do Toddlers Want?

Your soul. Just kidding. Toddlers want whatever pops into their heads at any given time. The problem is, these thoughts don't stop and they're going at rapid fire. This is why even though your toddler specifically asked for crackers, in the time it takes you to walk to the kitchen, pull the crackers out of the pantry, put the crackers on a plate, and walk back to your toddler, he now wants a piece of toast in the shape of Jay Leno's head. Did I mention that he is also heartbroken and furious that you have presented him with disgusting offensive crackers that have no meaning to him? He might feel the need to remove all clothing and cry on the floor, ultimately pissing himself, for 20 minutes even though you're late for work. WELCOME TO TODDLERHOOD.

Toddlers need movement. Have you ever looked at a two year-old running around and thought, "Are you on cocaine?" The reason why you're exhausted at the end of each and every day is because toddlers don't stop. You literally spend your entire day trying to keep them from breaking their faces on the floor as they run at the speed of light. Being a toddler is a never ending episode of American Ninja Warrior and the only prize is a visit to the emergency room.

Toddlers like to eat. And by eat, I mean graze and demand food. They like new, exciting snacks all the fucking time which will drive you insane by 10AM. Toddlers never finish their food. If you have a toddler who eats well, shut up about it and keep that information to yourself. Most of you will spend your days eating your toddler's scraps like some kind of Lululemon-wearing vulture. These calories don't count so do not worry about them. You eat those scraps to give your time spent making meals meaning. Try not to dwell on the fact that you're scarfing down trash.

Are Toddlers Crazy?

Precisely. Toddlers are nuts and will make you crazy, too. If you have a toddler in your home it's best to imagine that you live in a circus with an emotionally unstable cast. This way, when they throw a shoe at your head and rage vomit, you can shake your head and know that it has nothing to do with you and everything to do with them.

Toddlers can go from laughing to crying to screaming in a matter of seconds. There is no point in trying to keep up with their tsunami of emotions because as you're addressing one, the next one is already revving up to drown you. When you get overwhelmed by your toddler's feelings, it's best to just find a quiet corner to hug your knees and rock back and forth in. Your kid will seek you out and sit on your head but at least you tried. This is called yoga.

LIMITS AND BOUNDARIES

Toddlers need discipline. The only problem is that they're probably more committed to their wants than you are to following through. I'm going to offer up some controversial advice here: give them whatever will keep you from running away from home but stop right at the edge of Toddlers & Tiaras. You want to stay sane but you don't want to raise a Scott Disick.

Milk before bed? Who gives a fuck. If their teeth rot out of their head you can sleep easy knowing that a second set of grownup teeth are on their way. Baby teeth are like condoms- they're meant to be thrown away after use. They're like trainer teeth or disposable diapers. Keep them clean if you can but don't stress yourself. The #1 use of toddler teeth is to draw blood.

Is your toddler still wearing diapers at three? Who cares. Look at the bright side: at least you're not doing a mountain of pee pee laundry from potty training. The shame your kid will feel if they have to roll up to kindergarten in Pull Ups will take care of that problem for you.

Right now your job as a parent is to survive. You are in the trenches with a psychopath. Remember that. This isn't the time to play Holier Than Thou Parent. It's time to make it to the next day.

Ok, let's break for wine. You've earned it.

Toddlers And Grandparents

Nobody is enjoying you struggle with your little goblin monkey like your parents. Why? Because you were once a little asshole yourself. Your pain is their sacred revenge. Look closely at your parents when your toddler is melting down and you'll see satisfaction in their eyes. "Yes, my precious. Kick mommy in the face just like she did to me." Someone once said that toddlers and grandparents get along so well because they have a common enemy. You.

Nobody really gets over the toddler phase. Your parents will never admit but they hate you a little bit for what you did and take great joy in seeing you lose the battle with your own little fucker. I mean, doesn't the vision of your grown-up toddler begging their child/your grandchild to eat dinner make you smile? When your toddler is acting like someone with an acute case of the I-Don't-Give-A-Fuck-Itis in Target, characterized by trying to throw themselves out of the cart, just imagine being a grandparent yourself one day. Imagine taking your grandchildren out on a Saturday morning to Toys R Us and buying them loud electronic toys and filling them up on Mountain Dew/Pop Rocks before returning them home to your former toddler. How glorious will that be to hear them say, "Why can't you listen?" to their own child?

Toddlers love their grandparents with the love of a thousand suns. It is a pure love based on gifts, hugs, a no-rules environment and candy. Toddlers enjoy making you look like a liar in front of your parents so don't bother complaining to grandpa and grandma about how your pain in the butt is behaving.

"What? Jimmy isn't eating? He eats just fine with me. He just finished a Greek salad with feta and olives and is asking for spanakopita!"

Grandparents only know the sanitized version of their grandchildren because toddlers save their most terrible behavior for the people they live with full-time.

You do not have an ally with grandparents emotionally, but you do in terms of respite.

Drop off your toddler with the grandparents as much as you can. You may feel bad about doing this but you don't have to. Your child is not being as rotten with them as they are with you. They know better and

depend on grandparents as a source of refined carbohydrates and transfats.

The faster you can get comfortable with dropping off
your toddler with grandma and grandpa for entire
weekends at a time, the better your life will be. Don't
let your friends guilt you into thinking you're doing
something wrong. They're just jealous that you're getting time off to be a human person. You don't need to
warn your parents ahead of time that you will dropping off their little angel. Simply show up at their
house with your toddler for an unexpected surprise
visit to "see how they're doing." Wait for your toddler
and parent to be engaged in play or conversation and
excuse yourself to use the bathroom facilities. Sneak
out the back. Leave a garbage bag full of clean diapers,
wipes, and enough clothes for three days in the drive-
way with a $20 bill for expenses (be considerate). Drive
away like you just robbed a bank. Turn your phone
on silent. When/If you return and they protest mum-
ble something like, "Oh I thought you knew" or start
coughing hard until they drop it and ask you if you're
sick. Psychologists call this "Me Time."

Toddlers And Your Home

When you have toddlers it's normal for your home to
look like a tornado of pee diapers, plastic crap, cereal,
and mismatched socks. During the toddler years it is
vital that you abandon all hope of having a presentable

house. Your job is only to keep the child alive and some-what presentable. Get used to feeling crumbs in your bed at all times. That laundry mountain is normal. Piles of junk mail and random paper will be every-where. This is your new life.

Toddlers have no sense of self-preservation and will gladly climb, jump off of, and scale objects in your home as if you live on Mount Kilimanjaro. They will also attempt to eat coins, put forks in outlets, and hang glide off of dining room tables. Expect to spend every waking second keeping their soul inside of their body. You will NOT have time to clean. Even if you do clean, you efforts will be destroyed in a matter of moments as organized environments go against toddlers' primal natures. Cleaning hurts toddlers' sensibilities which is why as you do it, they will trail you destroying your progress.

Tips For Living With Toddlers

- Keep the vacuum cleaner out. There's no point in putting it away.

- Don't own anything made out of glass.

- Don't have fabric couches unless you love scrub-bing out bodily fluids until your fingers are raw.

- No carpet. Just hardwood. Better yet, try to live in the forest.

- No sharp edges unless you've always dreamed of having a child with an eye patch.

- Buy enough paper towels to fill a crawl space. Then get six more crates.

- All-purpose cleaner. Stock up.

- Clorox wipes. You need these. Poop.

- Get used to walking on crumbs. Wear socks or slippers or your bare feet will feel like they were wet dipped into a kitty litter box.

- Learn to love the sight of dishes piled in the sink.

- Find a living room covered in toys to be as beautiful as a sunset.

- Get used to living with your personal hygiene at an all-time low. You will smell like medical waste. You will smell like a month-old cream of crotch casserole sprinkled with Parmesan testicle cheese. Sometimes the wind will shift and you will catch your own scent and think, "Is there a dead raccoon nearby? Oh wait, that's just my privates."

Toddler Decor: If you have an actual bedroom for your toddler, this is fantastic. Decorate it with Elmo or whatever show they're into. If you're a contemporary parent or blogger, decorate it with leaves from your backyard spray painted gold and framed photos of places you've never been. Keep in mind that this bedroom will be primarily for time-outs. Toddlers do not sleep in their rooms. They fall asleep in there and wind up in your bed.

The Physical Toll Toddlers Take

Besides all of the weight you'll gain from drowning your nightly sorrows in take-out Chinese food and Tostitos, having a toddler will have other physical consequences.

1. Hair. Mothers, during pregnancy your child's bones grow strong from pulling minerals out of your body. After birth, your hair will start to fall out. During toddlerhood, this will increase. Your hair will also start to prematurely gray from both stress and fear that your life will always suck this hard. Parents showering is a serious offense in the toddler world so your un-conditioned hair will become brittle. Basically, expect to look like a scarecrow while your child is between one year and four years old. During this time, in family photos, you will look like a broom in yoga pants.

2. Skin. Because your toddler will have eaten all of your lotion, your skin will be at its driest. Since you live on a steady diet of refined sugar, toddler meal scraps, coffee, Red Bull, and alcohol, you will be vitamin deficient. Combined with the salt from the

tears you cry at night, your skin will be a hot mess. Dry, flaky, and sallow. Expect to rock the Disney witch look for at least three years. Pancake makeup would help but unless you're a Real Housewife who has time for that?

3. Clothes. You can always spot the toddler parents. They're dressed for the gym but have no membership. It's important to wear comfortable athletic wear while caring for a toddler because your day will be a marathon of getting shit for them. You will lose the will to change every day so just buy two pairs of black yoga pants and rotate them when your partner tells you that you smell like a rotten afterbirth.

4. Nails. It's perfectly normal for your nails to look like you dig graves for a living. It's almost poetic because at times it will feel as if your toddler is harkening your death. If your nails look like you lay pipe or pull up railroad tracks for fun with no gloves on, you're on the right track.

5. Shoes. Flats. Only flats. Only an idiot wears heels when you're taking care of a toddler who may break into a run at any time.

Toddler Preparedness Kit

If you're a new toddler parent, it can be helpful to make yourself a toddler preparedness kit. They don't sell these in stores so you'll have to fashion it yourself. Pull together the following items:

1. Baby Wipes: These aren't for your kid's butt, they're for yours. Since you won't have time to shower anymore unless you want to do it with a kid sitting at your feet starting at your genitals asking questions, it's good to keep a box of a wipes around to keep your nethers reasonably fresh. Moms, if you don't do this you'll get enough yeast infections to start baking vagina bread. Wipe from front to back unless you like antibiotics.

2. Aspirin/Tylenol: Sleep deprivation = regular headaches.

3. Vitamins: Try to remember to take these. You're going to need all the help you can get. Plus, if you get sick nobody will take care of you.

4. Netflix subscription: Say goodbye to seeing movies in the theater. You will watch them on Netflix four years after the general public. Due to constant falling asleep, it will also take you approximately three months to get through the average 90 minute movie. Because of this you will have no fucking idea what it's about.

5. Tic Tacs: Buy these in bulk and always have them on hand to bribe your kid to act right in

public. Tic Tacs are also a dentist-approved alternative to brushing your teeth.

6. Stickers: Sticker are currency in the toddler community. Yes, they'll end up in the most annoying places (like your butt crack), but they can also prevent grocery store meltdowns.

7. Smartphone with a good data plan: The Internet is your portal to the rest of the world. The people online are your only friends.

CHAPTER 2
YOU KNOW YOU HAVE A TODDLER WHEN

1. You know you have a toddler when you hate your spouse a little. Toddlers can destroy your marriage if you let them. The stress of living in an insane asylum with a child who makes you want to fall on your own sword will take a toll on your personal relationship. People without a toddler of their own will not understand how someone so cute will make you want to be single and living in a studio apartment with only a bottle of Jose Cuervo to keep you company, but this is the truth. Do your best to not let your little cock block tear your love life apart. You don't actually hate your spouse, it just feels like it because you hate life. Remember: You're in a warzone. You need back up.

2. You've no longer fantasize about being rich, famous, beautiful, talented, or any of the above. Your fantasies center around sleep.

You dream about being rested and floating away on a California King bed that you can lay in starfish formation in. Most people of think of sleep deprivation in terms of infants but toddlers have the potential to steal just as many Zs as their infant brethren. It's a hard truth to swallow but with a toddler you will be more physically and emotionally tired than you have ever been while also dealing with levels of twilight shenanigans that will astonish you on a nightly basis. Infants don't scream in your face. Infants don't run in to traffic.

3. You have become a shut in. Hopefully you have a backyard because other than work, you're going to lose your will to leave the house. It just won't be worth it anymore. Why deal with getting a toddler dressed, carseat drama, and a potential meltdown in public when you can just become a recluse? Groceries are available for purchase online.

4. You've ever had to drag a kid out of a store under your arm like a bundle of firewood in front of a crowd of gawking strangers. Good for you. Angry whispering can only get you so far. Sometimes you have to show a kid that mean business and abandon that cart of groceries. Don't abandon the wine, though. That's crazy. Pay for the wine.

5. You regularly open packages of food in stores to keep your baboon quiet while you shop. Don't worry; it's not shoplifting until you forget to pay for it.

6. You've ever had to alert a store employee to the fact that your kid has urinated on their floor. Hey, better a linoleum floor than a stack of neatly folded sweaters. Bonus points if your toddler has ever thrown up in public. On you. When you don't have a change of clothes.

7. You sometimes wish you had a time machine and a condom.

8. You have stress-induced heart palpitations. No, your child is not trying to kill you but they might by accident.

9. You've seriously considered starting a new life in a new city. If you do this, be sure to cut up your credit cards. They can track you.

10. You have more gates up in your home that the local zoo.

11. You know that sometimes "My phone is charging" is code for "I need you to lay off my shit and play with your own toys."

12. Your sex life has come to a standstill. Toddlers are natural birth control. Their antics

will cause your sex organs to shrivel into your body and seal off.

13. You've seriously researched sleep-away pre-schools and boarding school for two-year-olds.

14. You know more about the cast of Jake And The Never Land Pirates than your mom.

15. Every one of your cabinets has some kind of lock on it.

16. Bathtime in your house looks like an episode of Wipeout.

17. All four food groups can be found between your couch cushions.

18. You've had to say "Stop eating out of the trash" in the last 24 hours.

19. A small child has recently blown their nose into your shirt.

20. You would give your molars for a free, reliable babysitter. Who needs to chew meat when you can go out for drinks anytime?

21. You wonder if it would be creepy to ask teens on the street if they babysit.

22. You've ever fallen sleep with your eyes open.

23. You'd rather have a public colonoscopy than take your child into a store where glass items are displayed in the open.

Preparing Yourself For Typical Toddler Behavior

"Why don't toddlers listen?" Contrary to popular opinion, toddlers do not possess listening ears. They are unable to hear commands like "Stop" "No" and "Don't eat your boogers." Toddlers can only hear words that pertain to snacks. A toddler may not understand the words "Stay in your bed" but they will hear you chewing a Mentos from outer space.

Toddlers live by one simple idea: DO THE OPPOSITE

If you tell a toddler to wave to shop owner, they will stand there like a statue. If you tell a toddler to say hello to family member, they will stand there like a Precious Moments figurine. If you tell a toddler to keep breathing, they will hold their breath until they pass out. Toddlers live to disobey. Once you understand this you can control them through reverse psychology, or *mind fucking*, in layman's terms.

You need to think of your toddler as very bad roommate. They never pay bills, trash the place, eat all of your good snacks, and sleep with your girlfriend (have you been kicked out of your own bed yet?).

You're going to find yourself putting sentences together that you never could have imagined.

Things You Thought You'd Never Say That You Now Say As A Parent of a Toddler

1. I don't care how hungry you are, we don't lick eat peanut butter off of the sidewalk.

2. What have I told you about licking people?

3. I can tell you're pooping because your eyes are watering.

4. Toaster Strudels never go inside the DVD player.

5. Don't scratch inside of your diaper and then touch your face. You're going to get pinkeye.

6. Crayons do not belong in our nose, I don't care if you had an itch.

7. Your ears don't get hungry, please stop feeding them.

8. We don't pee on our friends. Even when we're mad, we don't pee on our friends.

9. There is nothing in the bathroom trash for you.

10. If you do that again, I'm canceling Christmas.

CHAPTER 3
FEEDING YOUR TODDLER

Toddler Food

Cooking for toddlers is difficult. I've made it easy with these recipes. Please know that your toddler may not eat them with his or her actual mouth. He may just touch the food and absorb a few nutrients through the pads of his fingers.

Breakfast is the most important meal of the day but also the time when most toddlers begin their mental terrorism. Do not ask a toddler what they want for breakfast because they don't fucking know. To make your life easier, stop thinking of meals in terms of "breakfast lunch, and dinner" and starting thinking of meals in terms of "calories this child needs to live."

Below are some recipes for toddler meals.

Savory Cheese Casserole

Ingredients:

Two slices of white bread. Look for the unhealthiest bread you can find. You'll want it as refined as possible. It should be white and soft as a pillow and contain no whole grains or detectable nutrients. This type of bread should have at least eight million grams of sugar and should spring back to the touch.

Grab a slice of cheese. Use processed cheese. It should almost resemble a neon orange piece of plastic.

Melt half a cup of butter into a pan. Place the cheese product in between the two slices of bread. Brown on both sides.

On a plate that your toddler is OK with (ask, don't assume), place the Savory Cheese Casserole and await further instructions.

Your toddler will let you know with a sharp howl if they would like the crusts cut off or if they would like the casserole in a special shape.

Toddler will then take 2-3 mouse-sized bites before asking for dessert. When you say no to dessert (because there is no fucking dessert with lunch), your toddler will cry so hard that they throw up the small amount of food they ate. Make yourself a vodka soda.

Rice Pilaf

Buy white rice. Not wild rice, not brown rice, not quinoa, WHITE RICE.

Place rice into a bowl that speaks to your toddler's mood.

Serve with enough butter to clog a giant's arteries. This meal should be as shiny and yellow as the sun.

Your toddler will be angry that the rice was served in a bowl, not a plate, because bowls are "for babies" today. Oh you didn't know? Learn to read your toddler's mind. In their fury, they will knock over the bowl of rice and it will fall on the floor. Sweeping up rice is next to impossible. It will congeal all around the broom. Just let it sit there until it gets hard. Give your toddler a cup of milk and put them to bed no matter what time it is.

Cereal

Pour your toddler's favorite cereal into a bowl. Add as much milk as they'd like. While they eat, pin to your "Healthy Recipes" and "Gluten-Free" boards.

Pizza

Spend $40 on pizza delivery. Listen to your toddler cry for thirty minutes about how pizza is all wrong.

Watch your toddler take a small bite of crust. Google "Can anger give you a heart attack?" Start the bedtime routine.

Pasta

Make enough pasta to feed a small village. Put pasta in a bowl with some butter. Watch your toddler massage pasta in their face and hair. Ask yourself why you even bother. Give toddler a bath.

Snacks

Toddlers believe with all of their hearts that you are their personal chef and request food pretty much 24/7. The fastest way to drive yourself crazy is with endless trips between the kitchen and living room couch.

The best way to give a toddler a snack is to throw a handful of Cheerios on the floor and let them serve themselves. Don't get your child addicted to bowls and spoons. Just throw down a sippy cup of milk in their direction and voila, you have a complete meal. Toss down some fruit or raisins if your toddler needs additional fiber.

If you opt to go the traditional route of having your child sit at a table for meals, please know that the food will end up on the floor anyway. You're wasting your time.

Vacuum up what's left at the end of the day or like any good cell phone plan, let those minutes roll over. Cheerios are even better the next day (or week). They age like fine wine.

Couch cushion snacks are also a great source of minerals as they are usually coated with dust and hair. Encourage your toddler to hunt for floor food while you read US Magazine. Pediatricians call this "bonding."

Toddler Puffs

Toddler puffs are sold in canisters and are always 50% full at the time of purchase. They cost between $50-100 a pop.

The only thing you need to know about crunchy toddler snacks on the market is that you're going to end up eating 90% of those suckers so pick a flavor you like.

Candy

Is candy bad for kids? Maybe. Is being annoyed bad for parents? Definitely. Give them some fucking candy. If you were born before 1985 your parents fed you a steady diet of processed meats, white bread, and pickles. Remember those American cheese sandwiches? The Kool-Aid? We survived. We didn't even know what organic apples were. A lollipop isn't going to kill your kid. Not unless the top comes off so give that pop a good pull to make sure it's on tightly.

Never give a toddler chocolate. This is inexcusable behavior. We don't waste chocolate on babies.

JUICE

It's time to calm down about juice, people. Some of you parents out there are acting like it's malt liquor. It's juice, not blue meth. Stop saying, "My child has never had juice," like your kid just won a Pulitzer. Remember the generation raised on Tang and its raggedy cousin, Sunny Delight? Yeah, that was us. I'm not saying you should pump your kid full of high fructose or even the 100% stuff, but quit with all of that sanctimonious bullshit.

Now to contradict myself: If you do bring juice into your home, know that it's the closest thing to giving your child an ecstasy pill. Your toddler will fiend for it hard. They'll pace like someone itching for a nicotine hit as you pour it and grab it out of your hands with legit desperation. Cut it with water if you want, but have you tasted your half-juice, half water concoctions? They taste like piss. You're the boss though.

MEAL TIPS

Mealtime with a toddler can only be described as a fat pain in the ass. It's best that you don't expect to eat.

You will spend the entire time getting up, fetching things from the kitchen, making empty threats about dessert, and blowing on food that is no longer hot.

Note: The first thing toddlers do when they sit down for a meal is need to urgently shit. This is universal. Even toddlers who have shown no previous interest in potty training will tell you they have to poop or that their diaper is full. This shit helps erase your appetite so that you can serve them like a slave during the meal. After wiping that little ass clean food will be the last thing on your mind. It's really hard to flush a burrito down the toilet and then sit down to some enchiladas.

When you're back from the bathroom with the scent of poo still in your nose, the next thing your toddler will do, if they are in a good mood, is begin to talk. They won't stop. They ramble on endlessly and ignore your attempts to direct their attention to their food. If your toddler is in a bad mood, they will cry and complain about the meal, flatware, and whatever else they can think of. Either way, no eating will be had.

If your toddler does eventually eat, it will be a few bites, no more. Most toddlers eat a thimble-sized amount of dinner before asking if they can have dessert.

It's best if you lie to your toddler and make them think fruit is an acceptable dessert. You and I know that fruit is never dessert but children aren't smart enough to know different. Giving toddlers fruit for dessert is good way to use up all of the produce left over from Instagram photo shoots.

Why do you want your toddler to eat? Because if they don't eat at dinner, they'll be ask for food at bedtime. The one thing you can do to make the sleep routine easier is fill up that toddler belly. Oh yeah and nutrients are good for them or something.

Frequently Asked Questions:

Can my toddler live on a steady diet of white carbs and milk?

Absolutely. Toddlers, like plants, get nutrients via photosynthesis. If your kid is on a food strike and slurping down whole milk in lieu of solids, don't get your panties in a wad. Unless your kid starts fainting, he'll probably be alright. Talk to your doctor. He or she might be able to get you a prescription that will make you happier.

Why won't my toddler try new foods?

Because it means so damn much to you and because toddlers also have highly sensitive taste buds. Flavors like eggplant and whole grains make them angry but Cheeto seasoning is just fine.

Why does it seem like my friends' kids eat better than my toddler?

Because your friends are either 1) fucking liars or 2) have an easier kid than you because God loves them more. Stop comparing and play the hand you were dealt.

Dirty Ways to Trick Your Toddler Into Eating

There are a few ways to get your toddler to ingest food other than milk and Ritz crackers.

1. Toddlers don't like to eat off of their own plates. It's too predictable. They much prefer raining on our own food parade by picking from your meal. When toddlers do this, it's their way of saying, "Motherfucker, I own you." If you've never tried to enjoy food while having a dirty, chubby toddler hand that has probably recently been up their butt reach into your plate and pull off your last slice of bacon, you're living the dream. Turn this fact into your advantage by loading up your plate with shit you actually want your toddler to eat and acting like you're in seventh heaven chowing down. Within moments your toddler will be at your side, begging for a piece of red pepper. Oblige them.

2. Ketchup. Toddlers like ketchup because it's 99% sugar. Serve it on everything. There are people on Pinterest who will try to get you to make low-sugar ketchup from scratch. Tell those people you don't have time for their bullshit science projects and give your kid the real stuff. Put it on broccoli, pizza,

potatoes, cheese, whatever you want your kid to eat. I believe they like it because toddlers are soul murderers and it looks like blood.

3. Bring in an extra kid. In the same way that hyenas enjoy picking apart a baby fawn carcass in community, toddlers enjoy eating together. The same toddler who spends family dinners crying will spend them eating if they have just one other toddler present. The more kids, the better they'll eat because it sets off the "orphanage response" which makes them worry there won't be enough food. It's not currently possible to rent a kid as a stand-in to get your toddler to eat, so you'll need to make some friends. Invite them over for lunch for the sole purpose of making sure your toddler gets a week's worth of calories in a single meal. Note: This doesn't work with siblings.

4. Melted Cheese/Velveeta. Velveeta is melted cheese's stupid step-cousin. It probably doesn't have any actual cheese but it is uniform in color and consistency and that's what matters most when you're two. Melted cheese can cover up all kinds of vegetables and meats. Go crazy.

5. The "one more bite" trick. Toddlers will always want to know how much food they need to pack into their gullets before you leave them alone and start the dessert course. You can use this to your advantage by repeatedly telling them they need to take "just one more bite." Because they can't count and are slow, they'll always think they're just one spoonful of casserole junk away from a brownie sundae. Keep the charade up as long as you can.

Don't feel bad if the only foods you can get into your toddler are crap. Most go through a stage where they will only eat foods that would get you kicked out of the Granola Mommies Club. Reframe that meal in your mind and **Ta da!** It's not as bad as you thought. Use the handy guide below.

New Names For Crappy Foods

Chicken Nuggets	Authentic Breaded Chicken Morsels
Pizza	Rustic Italian Flatbread With Cheese
Fish Sticks	Island Seafood Batons
French Fries	Gentle Potato Spears
Ketchup	Factory Fresh Tomato Aioli
Fruit Snacks	Dehydrated Fruit Carpaccio

SUMMARY

You can go ahead and make Pinterest-worthy meals if you'd like as long as you're OK with scraping them off of the floor. Organic chicken and cornmeal dumplings sound good on paper but nothing damages a psyche like spending four hours making a meal only to watch it get slowly pushed over the edge of a table with a child's index finger.

> **Sanctiparent:** *"This is terrible! No wonder kids these days are obese. My toddler loves salad and gobbles up arugula from our family garden!"*

> **Response:** *"Shut your damn mouth."*

A NOTE ABOUT RESTAURANTS

Do not take your toddler to a restaurant. There is no reason to do this. Even if the only things in your fridge are mayonnaise and beer there's still Chinese food delivery (get fortune cookies for the child) or a quick run through the McDonald's drive-thru. I'd even suggest making mayonnaise and beer soup before taking them out to eat. The alcohol will cook off. Never, ever take your toddler to a sit down restaurant unless it specifically caters to wild animals. If feral cats or rabid monkeys are not allowed in the restaurant, your toddler should not step foot in the establishment either.

Taking a young child in a restaurant will result in a nervous breakdown for all adults involved.

You will waste $12 on a child entree of macaroni and cheese which will go uneaten. You will take the macaroni and cheese home and attempt to feed it to your child the next day for lunch to recoup your money. Your child will refuse the macaroni and cheese over and over and you will end up eating it standing up in front of the fridge *three days* later.

You will spend your time trying to get your child up from under the restaurant table. As soon as the waiter arrives with your food your child will have to take the biggest, smelliest, longest, most explosive repulsive shit of their life in a public restroom. You will be responsible for wiping said shit off of their ass with the cheapest, thinnest toilet paper money can buy. The paper will be translucent and rip off one square inch at a time. There will be leak-through and you will experience poop on your hands 30 seconds before you're supposed to dive into a meal you paid good money for. You will return to your cold food with zero appetite.

You will spend the entire meal avoiding the hate gaze of other patrons as your toddler stares laser beams into their foreheads and speaks loudly.

You will ask your water for a cup of water for your toddler and they will return with a full-sized shatterable glass of ice water and hand it directly to your child as a way of saying, "Fuck you for bringing your kid in here."

One parent will spend their time walking the toddler around the restaurant and outside like a cocker spaniel while the other, luckier parent, eats alone.

If after all of this you still want to take your toddler to a restaurant, don't say you haven't been warned.

The only time it is recommended to take your toddler into a restaurant is if there is a zombie apocalypse and said restaurant is your family's agreed up on meeting location.

> **Sanctiparent:** *"My child is perfectly behaved in restaurants and never acts up. Maybe some of you should just take the time to raise better kids."*

> **Reponse:** *"Go fuck yourself."*

CHAPTER 4
ACTIVITIES TO KEEP YOUR TODDLER OFF YOUR BACK

You need to keep your toddler busy to avoid going stir-crazy. What is stir-crazy? This happens when a parent leaves adult reality and begins to enter their toddler's world. Symptoms include 1) identifying with cartoon characters, 2) becoming sexually attracted to members of The Wiggles, 3) forgetting what it's like to have a conversation with someone who isn't currently shitting their pants.

To avoid this condition, you need to regularly leave your home and keep your child from talking to you too much.

Parks With Toddlers: What You Should Know

All parents hate taking their kids to the park. We do it to wear them out and give them just enough social interaction to not end up living in our basements 20 years from now.

If you take your toddler to the park regularly and even push them on the swings even though what you really want to do is sit on the bench buried in BuzzFeed articles, good for you. You get a gold star for trying. Hell, even if you are buried in a BuzzFeed article or 6 (they're catchy, aren't they?) you still get a gold star because you haven't abandoned your child and that's how we define success around here.

Rules For Taking Asshole Toddlers To The Park

- Bring your own sand toys. Toddlers hate sharing and can you blame them? Sharing sucks and is almost impossible for a-holes. Pony up $6 and invest in some dollar store plastic shovels and buckets to keep your kid busy.

- Position your asshole away from small children. Toddlers like to dominate situations. Because of their small, puny size they often find themselves at a disadvantage. When a toddler sees a smaller child they will instinctively want to harm that kid by throwing sand directly in their face or kicking them in the back. This is normal. Avoid a lawsuit and confrontation with police by keeping your toddler away from children whose weaknesses they can sniff out.

- Bring lots of food. Toddlers are foraging beasts. They will happily and greedily follow around parents with snacks better than yours. To avoid the humiliation of your toddler begging strangers for food, bring at least 4 juice boxes, a bottle of water, fourteen string cheese, crackers they've never seen before, a jam sandwich, large bag of Ruffles potato chips, and two lollipops. You need two lollipops because one is going to be the wrong color. That one is for throwing in the sand.

Other Toddlers

Despite being similar in size and weight, toddlers do NOT have an interest in playing together. Think of it this way, do you like your coworkers? No. You want their lives to fall apart. Toddlers feel the same way about their peers. They engage in what is called "parallel play" which is when they sit close enough to occasionally try to steal each other's shit. Do not try to force a toddler relationship on your kid just because you have a parent-crush on another adult. This will be disastrous as your toddler will be able to sense your interest in another human being and try to sabotage it by spitting at them or slapping you in public. Like any jealous lover, a toddler's end game is not that you are happy or complete, but that you are isolated and devoted 100% to meeting their needs.

You did it. You're at the park. Take between 10-800 photos to let your Facebook friends know what a fantastic parent you are. Sit close enough to your toddler to prevent them from harming others but not so close that they can get sand on your phone.

Park Hazards

Water Fountain: Avoid the water fountain. By day it's a place to catch a cool, refreshing sip of water, but by night it's a sink where people without permanent addresses take whores' baths. If you feel OK with letting your kid drink water from the same spout wherein a drug dealer rinses off their genitals after receiving oral sex in lieu of payment, by my guest. Have fun filling that prescription for antibiotics. The only thing you should ever use the water fountain for is for water play in the sand. You can't get hand herpes. Go ahead and destroy the sand box by flooding it for your kid. You paid for it through your tax dollars so it's basically yours.

Razor Blades: Every now and then you'll hear on the news that some wacko has left razor blades around a park. Look up from your phone every hour or so to make sure you kid has all of their flesh. If they don't, finish your TMZ article and then call 911 or something. I don't know, I'm not a doctor. Apply pressure if you feel like it. I'm almost positive that fingers grow back anyway. They're like iguana tails.

Ice Cream Trucks: Ice-cream trucks prey on toddlers because their bottom line depends on your little mouth breather crying until they throw up so that you'll buy a $3 Popsicle that costs ten cents in the store. Some people will tell you that you should lie to your kids and tell them the ice-cream truck plays music when it's out of treats, but that won't work at the park. Herd mentality will kick in and your kid will see other kids stuffing their faces with high fructose delights. Go ahead and buy the ice-cream. Get a some soft serve for yourself and drizzle it with Baileys from your hip flask. You don't carry a hip flask? Weird. Get one then charge other parents a dollar each for a Baileys drizzle from your flask and you'll more than make back the money you spend on your kid's snow cone.

Annoying Neglected Kids: There's always that one kid at the park who you can tell hasn't been given affection since the nurse swaddled them on their day of birth. Initially you'll feel sorry for this kid as they follow you and your child around and try to join in on their games. These feelings will turn to annoyance when the orphan won't leave you alone. They'll ask questions, make demands (push on the swing, some of your snack, etc.) and keep trying to touch you as a way to get in their human contact quota. The parents of this minor are almost never to be seen. These kids are not homeless, they're usually well-dressed and groomed, but their a-hole parents are hoping that the world will do their job for them. Look, it takes a village but at the end of the day, your kid is your motherfucking kid. Handle that shit.

Leaving The Park

No matter how your toddler behaves at the park, you are required by law to take them home with you. This is an unfortunate part of the legal system that does not take into consideration parents' rights.

Toddlers hate leaving the park. When you arrive they usually assume that you live there now so having to say goodbye shakes them to the core. Pack light when you visit the park or use a backpack because you will have to carry your toddler out under your arm like a newspaper. Try not to pay attention to the looks from other parents. Move quickly. You will have to force your child's body into their carseat like you're pushing the trash down to avoid taking it out. Put some muscle into it. Don't park your car close enough for anyone to be able to read your license plate to Child Protective Services. Snitches are everywhere.

Toddlers & TV

Let's be honest: without television, most of you would have driven off a cliff by now Themla & Louise style. We're lucky to live in a time with a babysitter is just a click away. Experts will tell you that screen time is bad for kids, but do you know what else is bad for kids? Getting dropped off at a 7-11 with a backpack full of clothes. TV will keep you sane. Use it as much as you want. Remember, we set the bar very low around here. Our goal is to make it through the day, not to win trophies.

There are a crapload of options when it comes to entertaining your child with TV. Most television stations geared to toddlers have 24 hour programming or begin at 3AM because they know little assholes love to be up at all hours.

Whether you choose Nick Jr., Disney, or PBS, the most important thing to keep in mind is that your kid is hypnotized to the point where they stop asking for things.

Netflix is a wonderful option because it allows your kid to watch entire seasons of shows, like Bubble Guppies, at a time. Give your toddler a fresh diaper, cup of milk, and a box of crackers and look who now has a few hours of time to themselves? You are winning at this parenting game. Parent Expert Level: UNLOCKED.

Toys

Unfortunately, your toddler will probably get bored with their show eventually and want something from you. This is sad, yes, but you can prepare yourself by filling your family room full of so many toys that it takes them hours to make their way toward you.

We all say we're not going to be that parent whose living room looks like a Chuck E. Cheese threw up in it, but owning a massive amount of toys is key to surviving the toddler years. The toys aren't for your kid to play with, they're to serve as stumbling blocks around the house. Keeping your home like an obstacle course will help wear them out. Your house should look like an episode of Hoarders but will less rat droppings and more colorful shit.

The truth is that kids will play with their toys 8% of the time. The other 92% of the time they want your iPhone, the remote, Saran wrap, razors, mail, and other household items. The more inappropriate and inconvenient the item is for a toddler to have, the more they will want to hold it, love it, and call it their own. Don't spend too much money on fancy wooden Waldorf toys when at the end of the day, your toddler would be just as happy to unwrap tampons for an hour.

Prepare yourself by always having safe trash around for your sweet little rat bastard to take joy in. Fill it gum wrappers and watch your child's face light up. Paper. Beer bottles. The cardboard boxes McDonalds apple pies come in. Toddler love that shit. You could dump a box of recyclables over your toddler's head and they'd be in paradise because the bottom line is: toddlers love trash.

For your own sanity, never, ever buy toys that talk or sing. There's nothing adorable about hearing a toy say something ultra-creepy like, "Sing me a pretty little song" or "I love when you brush my hair" at 2AM in the dark as you make your way to the bathroom. You will shit your pants. During the day, toys that emit noise will grate on your nerves. There's a good chance that a well-meaning friend will buy your kid one of these pieces of toy chlamydia. Wait until you're alone and remove the batteries. When your kid grunts in protest, shake your head and look as confused as possible. You can also just throw that shit in the dumpster while they sleep. Never let your kid see you get rid of them. Toddlers are territorial animals. They are very averse to environment changes. Wait until 1AM and put all that crap in a garbage bag. Donate it and let it annoy a family in need.

IPADS, IPHONES, TABLETS

Toddlers quickly become addicted to electronic games. This is wonderful because while they're playing they will barely speak to you. Limit your little baby's screen time to no more than 6 hours a day for maximum intelligence. Get the free apps, not the educational ones. Your toddler will have so much fun decorating fake cupcakes and watching puppies roll around. Unfortunately, you'll sometimes want to be on your phone/tablet, too, or just want your toddler to take a break. Here are some lies you can use:

If you have an early riser, a tablet will keep them busy while you fall asleep on the couch. Never, ever download an application that your child needs your help playing. Life is hard enough.

Are you Oprah rich? No? Buy a case for your tablet. This should go without saying. Don't get a cute case, buy the kind that soldiers use- the type that keep electronics functioning in monsoons and can be dropped out of helicopters. Your toddler will destroy a $400 piece of hardware in a blind rage over a game not working correctly if you don't.

CRAFTS/PINTEREST

The very first craft your toddler does will take place during birth. They will rearrange your vagina into shredded meat. Once you're all healed and your kid is two, people will expect you to start doing crafts involving paper and crayons. This serves no purpose and will not make your child smarter, but it will give you a few photos to post on Facebook.

If you're into crafts, search Pinterest for "easy toddler activities." Chances are, a tutorial for handprints in the shape of turkeys or homemade playdough will pop up. Go for it. It will end in your child crying and eating most of that salt dough shit, but at least you'll have photos for when they're older and claim you never did anything with them.

If you're not crafty, avoid Pinterest during the toddlers years. That website is like a frenemy who is kind to your face but then tells everyone what a slut you were in college (and high school). Pinterest serves only one purpose: to make you feel like a horrible failure of a human being. No person has time to chevron paint a bedroom, make toddler lunches that look like cartoon characters, or build a sensory table. Have you seen those ice cube snack trays full of strawberry chunks, blueberries, cracker pieces, cheese, etc.? We all know that those might be cute but your hyena will flip it on to the floor faster than you can say "Failed IUD." Backyard carwashes with sponges and tubing...Pinterest assumes that you are a cross between June Cleaver, Martha Stewart, and a Home Depot employee, not a tired-ass, cranky parent of a toddler who is just trying to keep the kid entertained for a few minutes.

In conclusion, crafts are overrated and trying to do them with toddlers is what preschool teachers are paid for so leave it to the professionals.

Playdates

You absolutely need to have regular playdates if an asshole toddler lives under your roof. Playdates are not for socializing toddlers, their #1 purpose is to complain with your friends.

Don't invite just anyone in to your home. There are certain types of parents that will make your already terrible life worse.

Parents to Avoid:

1. Perfectionists: Look for toddlers wearing J Crew, designer hats, bow ties, and who say truly fucked up shit like "please" and "thank you." You don't want these assholes or their messed up parents in your home. They won't appreciate the Cheetos and Cheese Whiz platter that you put together for them and won't even let their spawn have a 10% real fruit juice box. These mofos will make you feel horrible about feeding your kid ketchup spaghetti for dinner and you don't need that in your life.

2. All-Natural Folks: You're only allowed to be gluten-free if you're a card-carrying member of the Celiac club, but these posers shun wheat just to be on-trend. Every conversation will turn into a speech about breastmilk, cosleeping, and vaccines so prepare yourself. These parents don't understand that "play-date" is code for "let kids wander the house and watch TV while we hang" and will want to interact with the children so don't bother getting close unless you're into the same things.

3. Authoritarian Parents: Ironically, hard-core parents usually have the worst behaved little a-holes of the bunch. These parents will

judge you for your empty threats and lack
of direction. Don't let them into your heart.
They thrive on the shame of others.

During the toddler years support is everything if you want to make it out mentally intact. Find some cool laid back people. You'll be able to spot them by their dirty clothes, Kool-Aid mustaches on their kids, and curse words.

Playgroups

Should I join an organized playgroup?

This depends. If you live in a place where it's next to impossible to meet other parents, join the playgroup. Find your rag tag crew of under-achieving misfits within the group. Keep in mind that playgroups usually have rules and expectations, but it's a worthy sacrifice to bring in a plate of store-bought muffins every now and then to avoid sitting with your toddler alone in your living room every day.

> **Sanctiparent:** *"I love taking my toddler to the park and playing with him. We stay for hours and build castles together. I don't get parents who don't want to be with their kids."*

> **Response:** *"You smell like shit."*

CHAPTER 5
GROOMING TODDLERS

Once you have a toddler each day will begin and end with a tango known as "changing clothes" or as many parents call it, "What The Fuck Is Wrong With You."

Despite your toddler having to get dressed each and every day of their life, they will act surprised as hell that you want to cover their nakedness. You may have to use MMA moves to keep your child still as you remove their 10lb pee-filled nighttime diaper. Getting their shirt over their big toddler head will be difficult. Look for shirts with wide openings. For some reason clothing manufacturers are under the impression that toddlers have normal sized domes. This is a lie. Toddler heads make up ¾ of their body weight.

Do your best to snake those flailing arms through the t-shirt holes. By now your toddler is screaming and may have tried to hit you. Your neighbors may be dialing 911 so if you hear cops at the door, answer promptly. Do whatever it takes to get pants on your lunatic. Socks will be difficult with them windmilling their legs, but try. Don't bother with shoes unless you have plans to leave immediately. If you put them on beforehand they will be removed and lost in the house for good. You will never find those things again. Actually, you will find one, which is worse.

Once your toddler is dressed, shadow them to make sure they don't strip off their clothes. Toddlers love to ruin a finished project as a way of flipping you off. If you can keep their clothes on their body for an hour after getting them dressed, you have a higher probability of not having to redress them.

Hair

Toddler hair isn't worth dealing with. If you have a boy, just try to keep it short. Use craft scissors while they're sleeping and aim for a respectable shape. If you have a girl, follow the same instructions. Toddlers hate getting their hair brushed and will howl like wolves if you attempt. If you have somewhere important to go like a funeral or modeling casting appointment, just spray your kid's hair with water. Wet hair usually looks better. I don't know what I'm talking about.

Teeth

Brush your toddler's teeth if you have energy for it at the end of the day. A second set will appear when they're older, so don't stress. The proper way to brush a toddler's teeth is:

1. Tell toddler it's time to brush teeth

2. Chase toddler around house

3. Pry mouth open

4. Try to weasel toothbrush in their mouth without scraping their gums

5. Apologize for scraping their gums

6. Explain that you can't put Band Aids on boo boos inside the mouth

7. Listen to toddler complain about how "spicy' bubble-gum-flavored-barely-toothpaste is

8. Hold back tears when toddler bites your finger

9. Tell toddler they have to open mouth more than 1 millimeter wide

10. Tell toddler not to swallow toothpaste

11. Watch toddler swallow toothpaste

12. Tell toddler to spit in the sink

13. Watch toddler spit on the counter

14. Yell to spouse that you need to tap out

Skin

Toddlers eat so much butter that their skin is always perfectly moisturized. If you ever run out of butter for say, corn on the cob, you can actually just run your warm corn down your toddler's arm and it will be nicely coated in a sweet and salty milk-based film. Go ahead. It's edible. Treat yourself!

What's ironic, is that toddlers will eat your lotion. Keep it on a high shelf. The odd taste will not stop your wildabeast from downing an entire bottle of Saint Yves Vanilla Orchard. Toddlers don't care.

Bathtime

Parents love bathtime because it always means that bedtime is near.

To prepare your darling for her bath, put on your full-length poncho because toddlers don't bathe, they splash, motherfucker. You're going to look like you're in a wet t-shirt contest. When toddlers bathe they act like they're a junior member of the summer Olympics diving team. Get ready. By the time you're done your bathroom floor will have a few inches of water on it. The good news is that wiping all that water up counts as washing the floors.

Buy bath toys if you want but what toddlers really love to play with are kitchen utensils. The weirder the utensil (couscous sieve, egg smasher), the more likely that your kid is going to need that shit in their bath on the immediate. Give it to them. Throw in a couple Tupperwares, too.

Kids usually have so many toys in their bath by the time you go to take a shower, it'll be like cleansing yourself inside of the dollar store. The amount of crap in on your tub floor will rival that of your garage. Try not to slip or you could end up with a spoon up the ass (unless you're into that then slip away.)

You should know that it's perfectly normal for a-holes to cry about taking a bath and then cry when they have to get out. Don't try to wrap your mind around that. It is what it is. Never blame yourself for your toddler's shortcomings. You gave them life.

Note: Toddlers love bubbles. While the water is running, squirt in some dish soap.

CLOTHES

Look, we all know how fun it is to dress up toddlers. Go all out if it makes you happy. There are a lot of options these days for clothes for your kid.

Target: $4 pants and shirts. Enough said.

Etsy: This is the place to shop if you don't mind spending $140 on an ensemble. Be aware that if you make Etsy your go-to store your child will end up looking like some kind of mayor hobbit or Dr. Seuss character. None of this shit is machine washable because it was hand-sewn by a raw vegan lunatic living in Oregon who doesn't even own a fucking washing machine.

Walmart: More cheap clothing. Always buy one size up so your child's clothes never fit correctly. It'll make you feel like a planner.

Do your best to befriend a parent with a child 1-2 years older than yours. Beg for their hand-me-downs with no shame. If these parents don't plan on having any more kids, have expensive taste for quality clothes, and have no nearby family to hand off items to, you've just won the lottery. Do whatever it takes to keep these people happy. Surprise them with wine. Go on and on about how poor you are and how cold your child is every winter.

Other Grooming Tips:

Try to clean your toddler's neck every now and then. If you don't a black ribbon of dust and grime will accumulate Oliver Twist style. Get behind their ears with a damp washcloth and give it a solid wipe. You may have to hold them down to do this. Toddlers like to be dirty.

It's fine if your toddler smells like farts and old milk. They all kind of do. That fresh baby smell is gone.

CHAPTER 6
TODDLERHOOD 101

Why exactly is having a toddler so hard? Because they can't be reasoned with. See, adults are used to dealing with people who they can talk stuff out with or at least post a passive aggressive Facebook status to work out issues.

This is how an average conversation goes with a toddler.

> **Dad:** *"Hey buddy, we need to get dressed so that we can leave for the park."*

> **Toddler:** *"I want to go to the park."*

> **Dad:** *"I know. So let's get dressed."*

> **Toddler:** *"No, I want get dressed go to park now."*

> **Dad:** *"But you're naked. You can't be naked at the park."*

Toddler: (Crying and screaming, maybe pissing the floor at the same time splashing urine on father, accidentally kicks dad in the nuts) *NO GET DRESSED PARK! NO SHOES PARK! NO PANT!"*

At this point the dad is wishing he'd masturbated in the shower instead of conceiving this crazy mofo.

Toddlers look like babies, but don't get it twisted, babies are pretty easy to dress. Babies don't try to hit you. Babies don't lower your self-esteem by commenting on how big your ass is and asking if you have to buy clothes at a special store for said large ass.

Toddlers walk through life like we all wish we could: confident, demanding, and 100% positive that they are the center of the universe. They can kick their father in the testicles and feel nothing. They love to laugh. They love to destroy expensive cosmetics and fingerpaint with long-wear lipstick. Toddlers love to render electronic devices useless. They enjoy making debit cards and keys vanish into thin air. They like to permanent marker on shit.

Toddlers live that #thuglyfe better than any of us could even try to because toddlers. don't. give. a. fuck. The quicker you understand that the better. Repeat after me: Toddlers don't care.

CHAPTER 7
DAYCARE, PRESCHOOLS AND NANNIES

Working parents or stay-at-home parents who have just had enough will find themselves in a position to look for daycare or preschool for their toddler. A lot of parents feel judged for putting their toddler in daycare or preschool. You should never pay attention to the opinion of someone who isn't currently paying your bills. If you need, or just want, to have someone else take care of your toddler while you earn a living, that's your right.

Here's what you need to know when searching for a daycare/preschool:

1. When it comes to price, approach it the same way you do a wine list in a restaurant; you want cheap, but not the cheapest. Choose the one second from the bottom.

2. Look for a preschool with bright colors and crafts around. This tells you that they're committed to bright colors and having crafts around.

3. Definitely find one that serves meals and doesn't require you to pack a lunch.

4. It should smell kid-bad but not sewer-bad in the daycare. If it smells like raw sewage, don't select it unless they give you a raw sewage smell discount.

5. Ask about their commitment to parental involvement. If they want parents to be involved don't choose that one. Ain't nobody got time for that.

6. Ask them if they have any kind of fundraisers. If they say yes, get up and leave. Why should they need to fundraise when you're paying so much?

AFFORDING PRESCHOOL

Preschool is damn expensive. It would be better if it cost an arm and a leg than actual money because then you'd be able to get two kids through before you were left without appendages. Most families cannot afford preschool but put their kids in it anyway and just try to not cry when the overdraft fees start rolling in.

Here are few tips for making extra money for preschool/daycare:

1. Turn tricks.

2. Sell the gold in your fillings.

3. Become a web-cam sex object person.

4. Sell scrap copper you find in your neighbor's garage.

5. Sell blood plasma.

6. Start cutting hair in your kitchen. If you don't know how to cut hair make sure you get paid up front.

7. Don't pay and just show up to preschool and drop your kid off. You'll only get away with this for 2-3 days.

8. Buy Carter's brand stuff at Goodwill and sell it on eBay.

9. Eat Hamburger Helper for dinner every night (don't use hamburger).

10. Get some dirt on the preschool director and bribe them.

Things to look out for:

You DON'T want a daycare that will let your kid nap for six hours in the afternoon. They're not getting paid to supervise sleepers. They're getting paid to be annoyed by children. All that rest will bite you in the ass come bedtime.

What Can I Expect With A Toddler in Preschool?

Art: You're going to get a lot of arts and crafts sent home. It's going to look mediocre and overwhelm your living spaces. Use it to build fires in the winter but don't let your toddler see catch you doing this. To toddlers, nothing is trash, especially not crap they're scribbled on. You might be thinking, "How many hand-prints on paper do I have to keep?" If your toddler were in charge the answer would be, "ALL OF THEM." Pin-terest parents take photos of all of the art or organize them in giant bins in the garage. What for? You think one day that shit will be worth something? Or your child will take all that crap to college with them? Keep 1 or 2 to prove they had a childhood, frame another for grandma for the holidays (this gift costs next to noth-ing), and put the rest at the bottom of the recycling.

When you have a toddler you have to smuggle their art out of the house the way people bring in snacks to the movie theater or drugs into a nightclub. Get creative. Between the boobs, in your boots- do what you have to do.

Snack Parent: You may be asked to bring in the occasional meal. Pay attention to any allergy notices. While it's fine to be lazy, it's not cool to do it at another kid's expense. If you can't make a peanut-free cupcake then break a $20 and go buy some. Bring in a premade grocery store fruit plate. Do not let overachieving parents make you feel bad for not creating multi-colored rainbow surprise cookies with M&Ms on the inside. Ain't nobody got time for that shit. Even if you did have time, why would you waste it making treats that will literally turn into toddler shit a few hours later when you can watch Netflix or take a well-deserved nap?

Multiple Personalities: Your toddler will have a daycare personality and a home personality. The daycare personality will be better because they know 100% that you won't murder them for their bad behavior but the same can't be said for a stranger teacher. Toddlers are smart animals, they know that if they pulled the shit they do at home their teacher might snap on them. When your toddler's daycare teacher says stuff like, "Leo is such a good kid!" when you know Leo is rotten to the core, don't challenge them and try to prove them wrong because that just makes you look crazy. Yes Leo woke you up this morning by straddling your head and pissing in your face, and yes when you were rifling around for your cell phone in your handbag you pulled out a turd Leo had left put in here, but just let it go.

Common Questions:

Dear Asshole Whisperer, My kid has a fever. Can she still go to preschool?

That depends. Will you get fired if you don't go to work? Yes? She can go to preschool. Give her some Tylenol. If they call you pretend you didn't know. Kids in daycare are sick pretty much 24/7 building up their immune systems. If you keep your kid home every time they feel like a cinnamon bun fresh out of the oven, they'll miss more days then they'll actually attend. Now if your snowflake is barfing up their guts, lethargic, and has turned a shade of pea-green, you might want to call in to work.

There is a biter in my kid's preschool class. What should I do?

Teach your kid to bite back. Let your kid know that in your house you don't start fights but you always finish them. If your kid is the biter, file down their teeth.

Why does preschool cost so much?

Would you want to be a preschool teacher? 'Nuff said. Having to put 20 kids down for a nap is going to cost you. Plus you have to wipe the butts of kids you that aren't in your custody probably sucks.

Should I feel bad about putting my kid in day-care?

No. Do what you need to do in life. Haters gonna hate. Speculators gonna speculate. Life ya life.

Note: One terrible aspect of preschool and daycare is that it will put you in direct contact with parents who are doing better than you are. During drop-off and pick-up you will notice that there are parents who drive very expensive vehicles, are physically attractive, fit, and dressed well. We call these people bitches (applies to males and females) and avoid them. If it helps, imagine that their personal life is in shambles.

Look for the parents who look like they were just released from prison: unshaven, hunched over, afraid of sunlight, confused, shoes on the wrong feet, etc. These are your people.

CHAPTER 8
TANTRUMS

Everyone has seen a toddler lose their damn mind over an orange having seeds, someone putting them into their carseat before they were ready, or the sky being an ugly shade of blue. Your toddler WILL throw a tantrum at some point in time.

Your response to the tantrum will depend on A) how tired you are and B) who is watching.

If you're in public, you'll probably try to put on a "good parent" show on account of the witnesses. If you're in private, you will most likely ignore the tantrum entirely and walk into the kitchen for anther spoonful of medicine (Nutella) while your nutbag writhes on the ground screaming with tears running down their blotchy face as if they just lost someone they love.

You cannot talk a toddler down from a tantrum no more than you can talk a tornado down from destroying lives. When a toddler is going full ape, you get in your storm shelter and wait it out. Tantrums serve one purpose and one purpose alone: to strip your nerves like a wire so that you'll give the little mofo what they want. The more you give in, the more tantrums you'll get so become good at tuning them out. Learn to distance yourself from reality and find a happy place to reside in. Only idiot parents whisper: "Hey buddy, hey, hey there, hey little buddy," while their kid loses their fucking mind. They can't hear you. Try reflecting their feelings if you feel up to it but no one will blame you if you don't.

CHAPTER 9
TWO YEAR OLDS

Terrible twos. If you say so. Two year olds are as cute as your kid is ever going to get. They're trapped between babyhood and kid-hood and it's a beautiful thing to behold. Is there anything cuter than a two-year old Tweedle Dee stumbling around?

Depending on your personal destiny, your 2T might be a sweetheart or a raving lunatic. However they are, please know that their behavior will go downhill from here. While they might not be in full toddler mode now, they will often start to show glimpses of what lies ahead.

You may notice your two-year old who was sleeping fantastically up until now start to resist going to bed. They might also start waking up in the middle of the night or at 4AM ready to start the day. This is a warning.

You've been thinking that you're a pretty amazing parent, have you? That maybe you lucked out? Hahaha. Wait. Just wait.

If you have a two-year old who is already batshit crazy and exhibiting many signs of assholery, as least the suspense is over. Despite your 2T being able to walk, they will probably demand to be carried everywhere. Tots don't care if you're carrying $500 worth of groceries and their baby sibling, they want up and they want it now. Prepare to spend hours of your life watching your toddler sit on the ground pretending like their legs stopped working The Secret Garden-style. Wait them out. You only have one back and if you waste it lugging around a walker you won't be able to enjoy having an empty nest one day. Spend big bucks on toddler carriers if you'd like but know that that money could also be going toward margarita mix.

2Ts are next to impossible to understand and feel self-conscious about how much they suck at speaking. This is why being asked to repeat themselves sends them into a rage. Pretend to understand their gibberish or you'll get bitch slapped. Two year-olds are cute but never, ever mistake their elf good looks for kindness.

CHAPTER 10
THREE YEAR OLDS

Age three is when your toddler enters full asshole mode. The only sign of that docile little baby you gave birth to will be in their face while they're sleeping. Three-year olds spend most of their awake time crying, crying louder, and scream crying. When they're not doing that they're whining and making a scene. Three-year olds have only one goal: to make you look like a bitch-ass punk in public. Once you know this, you'll pick your battles. Pick none of them. Don't engage in arguments with a three-year old because if you're yelling or explaining, they've already won. Three-year olds are power hungry despots who take pleasure in seeing you become unhinged. Keep a flask close at hand and take a hit whenever you feel your blood pressure rising.

It's important to know that three-year olds believe that they are victims. They believe that they are royalty. They believe that everything they want, whether it is a new Rainbow Dash My Little Pony or a grilled cheese sandwich with no cheese and no crust, should be delivered immediately on a golden platter.

When you disappoint a three-year old they descend into a manipulative rage and their anger knows no bounds. A 3T will cut you where it hurts. Their impressive vocabulary will string together all sorts of insults. Age three is when you will most likely wonder if you have given birth to the anti-Christ. If a three-year old could cut off your finger with a katana as a punishment for putting their toast on the wrong plate, they would. Not because they hate you, but because they are emotionally unstable beings who do not live further than the present moment. Three year-olds don't just carpe the diem, they carpe your will to dress yourself, eat nutritionally dense foods, and take them anywhere. They do best in groups with other 3 year-olds. In a community of their peers, these toddlers will create complicated Lord of the Flies hierarchies rich with unspoken rules/contracts. Don't try to make sense of it, just enjoy that they aren't giving you hell.

Note: Avoid eye contact with three year-olds when they are hungry or tired. Like violent dogs, they assume you are challenging them and will charge. Too many people have lost nipples to the teeth of three year-olds. Too many.

CHAPTER 11
FOUR YEAR OLDS

Right now you're wondering if a 4-year old is a toddler. Kinda. Four-year olds believe that they are rockstars. Divas. Celebrities. They operate on the assumption that if you don't bow down to them it's because you're jealous. Four year olds are a cross between Charlie Sheen, Lindsay Lohan and Stephen Hawking: they don't seem to learn from their mistakes, are highly unpredictable, but show sparks of pure genius.

Four year olds love to argue, however, they are not at all committed to making sense or following logic. Four year-olds are like three year-olds but better at pressing your buttons. Their lungs are also more developed so their screams carry farther.

Since you know what matters to them now and they understand cause and effect, it will be easier to tailor custom threats to control their behavior. Bribes work much better with a four year-old as well because they now understand the purpose of money.

Try to get your four year-old into some kind of preschool or military academy. They're surprisingly good at following instructions when given by people that don't love them. If you're at home with a four year-old all day try to be outside. Nature will help you co-parent. Nature will share custody of your child. Four year-olds indoors are known to be clingy and will constantly be trying to re-enter the womb or if you're male, will try to meld their skin to yours. This age group goes back and forth between teenager-like antics and behaving like a newborn. You never know which side you're going to see which will cause you to drink more than ever from the stress.

CHAPTER 12
THE COST OF RAISING A TODDLER

Toddlers don't need much in terms of material belongings but you'll still spend a fortune on them. The bulk of the money will go toward paying people to keep them busy. After that, you'll spend money on Pull-Ups which if you didn't know are $18/diaper. I say diaper because that's what a Pull-Up is. Don't kid yourself. Just because the sides are a little more permanent in nature, doesn't mean your kid isn't still pissing and shitting themselves in a plastic bag. Pull-Ups cost so much because they sell the illusion that you are that much closer to having a potty-trained kid when in reality you're not closer at all. Pull-Ups are a lie.

Toddler clothes add up quickly. Now that you've stopped doing laundry, you're going to need to buy clothes every time you're in Target. Cheap $4 shirts and $20 no-brand sneakers can put quite the strain on a budget when they're purchased weekly.

You're going to spend a considerable amount of cashola on toys. Plastic outdoor playhouses that click together and cause large patches of your lawn to die under it, mini see-saws, $5,000 backyard swing sets, play tables, and countless blinking/flashing toys. Why do we buy them? Because you hope that eventually you'll find that toy that your toddler loves so much that they stay away from you for more than 15 minutes.

Each toy purchase is a gamble for a moment of peace. They're like lottery tickets. You know you're going to lose but it's fun to try.

The main costs associated with having a toddler will be:

- Adult Beverages

- Netflix Subscription for Relaxation Purposes

- Antidepressants

- Preschool/Childcare

- Cleaning Supplies

- Replacing Broken Electronics/Mobile Phones

- Repairing Gashes on Leather Couches

- Re-carpeting Your Home

- Deep Cleaning of Car on a Monthly Basis

You will also spend a large amount of your family's income on take-out food. It's easier to deal with meals being constantly rejected when you aren't the one cooking. Plus, the Witching Hour is NOT an ideal time to cook. You are at the lowest energy of the day and your toddler is at their assholiest. It's much easier to have someone deliver some crappy food than try to cook with a human puppy hanging off of your leg whining like Bruno Mars.

Toddlers are expensive.

CHAPTER 13
NATURAL BIRTH CONTROL

NATURAL BIRTH CONTROL METHODS

If you have a toddler you probably aren't trying to have another kid. Or maybe you are because pain is just your thing. In addition to your chemical or latex birth control, nature has also provided ways to keep yourself from reproducing during this trying time.

Working Dads: Coming home and hiding in the bathroom or garage while your loving partner makes dinner with a toddler cries under her feet is a very effective birth control method. It guarantees that no sexy time will be had. The only thing that will go down regularly in your life is the sun. Oh you need, alone time? Chances are your spouse doesn't even know what the fuck that is anymore. When you get home, wash your hands, go pee, change and jump right into the madness you helped created. Alone time. You think this is motherfucking game? If you ever want to get head again, pull your weight. The quickest way to get cut off from naked Twister is to act like working outside of the house makes you exempt from equal parenting. Mofo.

Stay-at-Home Dads: Most likely your toddler has already broken your spirit. Being a stay-at-home dad is no joke. Oftentimes, the moms at the park treat you like a potential sex offender at a time when adult conversation is critical to your emotional health. If you're anything like the stay-at-home dads I know, your libido has been trampled into the carpet like a stale Goldfish cracker and you have no desire to add to your brood.

Stay-at-Home Moms: The stench that will come from your crevices because you haven't showered due to staying home with a toddler all day also repels sexual partners and will keep your womb barren.

Working Moms: Undoubtedly, you miss your toddler during the day, but no one will think badly of you if you also admit that after a long day of dealing with terrible bosses and even worse coworkers the last thing you want to do is argue about broccoli with someone younger than most of your moles. The sheer exhaustion from balancing (and being judged for) an outside-of-the-house job is enough to pause ovulation.

Sex

If you do opt to engage in sexual relations while the parent of a toddler know that you'll have some hurdles to jump through.

Hurdle #1: The smell. I just want to take a minute to each out to the good people at Febreeze. Why have you not developed a spray that people can use to make their privates smell like wildflowers? You've done such a good job making junkyard homes smell clean, it's time to toss parents a bone here and make some kind of body spray that serves as a "shower in a bottle." Feel free to use that slogan.

Because you lack the time and will to shower, one or both parents of a toddler will walk around looking relatively normal but the inside of your underwear will smell like a dive bar bathroom urinal cake. Since sex tends to expose these crevices, the love den will take on the odor of an outhouse which doesn't exactly make for a sultry environment.

Solution: Have sex with the windows open. Don't turn on any fans which will just waft the odors directly into your nose. Keep a candle lit to burn off ass/vagina/penis vapors.

Hurdle #2: Fatigue. You're tired as hell from pulling nickels out of your toddler's mouth and scraping food into the trash. The last thing you want to do is assume the position. Also, when you've had a small child crawling all over you all damn day, holding your hand, sitting in your lap while you eat dinner, the last thing you want is another person all up in your business. By the end of the day, parents who hang out with toddlers during daytime hours or work just want to mentally check out and not have anyone within 1ft of them.

Solution: Masturbation! Just kidding. There is no solution.

Hurdle #3: Your cockblock toddler. Toddlers hate knowing that you have relationships outside of them. They are experts when it come stop sibling prevention. You've probably noticed by now that just as you're feeling frisky and have convinced your partner to drop their undies that your little one, who you thought was asleep, lets out a Adam Levine-style falsetto note.

Solution: Turn off the baby monitor so you can't hear your child's cries. This could backfire terribly so use at your own risk. If your toddler sleeps in your bed, you have no choice but to get it on in the living room or backyard. Hopefully you have a high fence.

If your toddler is in a crib they can't get out of and you do decide to play through, more power to you. Just make sure you have a lock on your door lest you look up from your passionate gorilla love making to see a 2ft tall human curiously staring at the business side of your private parts. There's no unseeing that and it will end up being relayed in great detail to a preschool teacher the next day.

CHAPTER 14
CAILLOU

If you're unfamiliar with Caillou, he is the leader of the toddler community. He is the spirit animal by which they take orders. Caillou is who every toddler aspires to be. He's a whining shit stain of a kid who despite having no redeeming qualities, not even physical attractiveness, still gets everything he asks for. If most of us were Caillou's parents, we would have dropped him off at grandma's house and moved to Jamaica. That child is a demon's spawn. His whine could strip paint. His cries generate no sympathy in parents, only rage.

Parents, have you noticed that as your child watched Caillou they began whining more? If you have not gotten your child addicted to this degenerate of a television show character, ban it in your home. Even if your child loves the program, ban it. Just ban it all. Nobody needs that little kidney stone in their life. He will poison your child's soul. While I don't have proof, I believe with all of my heart that Caillou is the work of the underworld.

One of the worst parts about Caillou is that his parents seem oblivious to his assholery. They reason with the monster, give him treats, take him on trips, when all that little pile of talking vomit deserves is solitary confinement. I have a theory that his parents are taking powerful sedatives making them immune to Caillou's behavior. It's also making them immune to the fact that they are constantly wearing each other's clothes. The only person we need to pity in this situation is the cat and his sister Rosie for being born into this family.

Since we're on the topic of toddler television shows we may as well tackle Max and Ruby. This series tells the tale of two bunny siblings. It's never stated outright that the female elder sister, Ruby, killed their parents, but it's implied. The rabbits are now raising themselves with a little financial help from their grandmother. Her silence was bought with threats. The purpose of this show is to teach toddlers how to mentally abuse their friends and family. Ruby treats Max like shit but I'm 99% sure he's going to snap and make a pot pie out of her in upcoming seasons. Cannibalism aside, I support his decision. She has it coming. Hopefully he goes full Dexter and takes out Caillou, too.

Handy Manny is also a popular show for youngsters. It's a program featuring Manny, a struggling handy man whose addiction to hallucinogens is spiraling out of control. Manny is convinced that his tools frequently come alive and argue amongst themselves. Because of his problems, his neighbors take advantage of his decreased awareness and make him work on shit for free.

Spongebob Square Pants is a show designed to help parents who need a reason to rip their eardrums. The sound of this character talking and laughing has been the cause of every major world war.

Bubble Guppies is a the tale of 4-5 sperm living in some guy's balls. They sing, dance, and learn lessons.

PBS is for parents who want to hypnotize their kids with TV but feel guilty. Sesame Street is definitely educational and not completely unbearable. Every once in awhile a celebrity will come on and act like they invented happiness, but besides that, it's not bad. This network broadcasts Caillou to children though so we have to question their judgment.

CHAPTER 15
HOW DO I GET MY TODDLER TO LISTEN TO ME

You don't. Toddlers don't listen. They can't hear anything above a low drone of their innermost desires. Toddlers, much like show dogs, communicate through rewards and punishment. The reason your empty threats don't work is because toddlers are equipped with BS-O-Meters that rival CIA agents. They know when you're lying and act up accordingly. When dealing with these pint-sized gangsters, it's important that you say what you mean and you mean what you say at least 20% of the time. The random times you do follow through are enough to throw them off and instill in them that you're a wildcard. Anything less will be tested in the most annoying of ways.

Common Empty Threats

You: *"I'm going to tell your father."*

Toddler: *"No you won't, you're going to tell Facebook. Do you think I care what your* *raggedy friends think of me? By the time daddy gets home you'll be so thankful to have someone to throw me at that you'll spend the rest of the evening in the kitchen making yourself drinks and forget all about this moment."*

You: *"If you do that one more time you're going to be in big trouble!"*

Toddler: *"If I do this one more time you're going to get so mad that you'll change the scenery. The mall? The park? Starbucks where you'll get a venti mocha frappucino with three extra espresso shots because I woke up at the ass crack of dawn and a chocolate cookie the size of my head? Why not."*

You: *"Do you want me to call Santa?"*

Toddler: *"Actually, yes. Tell him that I've already broken all my toys and am going to need fresh ones. You're not kidding anyone, I know Santa is coming no matter what. You loved watching me open those presents more than I loved playing with them."*

Do you see where we're going with this? Toddlers know we're lying when we threaten them. Talk means nothing to a toddler. They come from the streets. And in the streets, actions mean everything. When dealing with an asshole, you have to put your money where your mouth is. The best we can do is actually put them in time-out and let them experience the earth-shattering horror that is having to stay still for a few minutes while the world continues to spin around them. I don't recommend threatening to burn their stuffed animals unless you're going to videotape that shit and send it to me. Burning their toys is cruel. It'd be funnier to stomp the shit out of their LeapFrog tablet Office Space style, but this might land you in some kind of government mandated parenting class.

CHAPTER 16
HOW TO NOT DIE INSIDE

Spending your days and nights with a child who gives you stress headaches can make you wonder if having kids was the worst mistake you ever made. It wasn't. Having kids while not being rich enough to afford a nanny was the worst mistake you ever made.

There are ways to deal with the pain of having a child who makes you want to scream "WHAT DO YOU WANT FROM ME" repeatedly while hitting your head against a brick wall. No, I'm not talking about self-help books about spirited (ie. devilish) children or spending more time outside, I'm talking about alcohol and re-fined carbohydrates.

Alcohol, chips, and candy will get you through the toddler years like a champ. We touched on this in an earlier chapter but I want to stress the importance of making sure your home is well stocked with these life-saving items.

Every parent of a toddler needs their own Night Stash. What is a Night Stash? It is a treasure box full of items such as Skittles, Hershey Bars, Doritos, and tortilla chips. Maybe you live in Colorado and your night stash contains a blunt or two. We don't judge around here. Do not, I repeat, DO NOT keep these items in the kitchen where your toddler can sniff them out like one of those truffle-hunting pigs. Especially if it contains a roach (see above about government mandated parenting classes). Your Night Stash should always be stored in your room as it will be consumed in your bed between the hours of 8PM and 2AM.

Keep your Night Stash in a grocery bag in your closet or in your nightstand if you don't think your toddler will get into it. Knowing that these goodies exist is key to making it through the day with your sanity intact.

Do not attempt to restock your stash while grocery shopping with your children. Toddlers can sense deliciousness and will attempt to steal your hard-earned food. Pick up items in secret whenever you can and shuffle them into your bedroom while your hot mess is hypnotized by Playhouse Disney.

Consuming Your Night Stash

While it can be difficult to wait, your Night Stash will taste 99.99% better if eaten while your child is asleep. The last thing you want is a toddler wandering into your room when you have a Reese's half-stuffed into your mouth.

What can I enjoy while I'm waiting for my child to pass out?

Alcohol! Kids know that liquor is off limits so you're free to partake in their presence with no risk of having to share. Happy Hour generally starts at 5PM in the mainstream world but for parents of toddlers, as long as you know you don't have to drive anywhere you're good to go.

You know your limits. The good thing about having children present means you're never actually drinking alone. Don't overdo it or you just might end up the subject of a Lifetime Original Movie and nobody wants that.

Drinks Recipes for Parents of Toddlers

The Why Aren't You Potty Trained

In a clean baby bottle, measure 2 ounces of Baileys Irish Cream. The ounce measurements on bottle are designed to make pouring liquor more accurate. Pour into a coffee mug. Drink straight. Repeat if you want.

The Why Isn't Your Dad Home Yet
(usually consumed between 5:15-6PM)

Uncork a nice bottle of cabernet sauvignon. Pour it into a measuring cup, Tupperware, or empty, clean margarine container. Sip on the couch while your child throws the toys you just put away out of the box. For every minute late your spouse is, dedicate a dollar toward a future bottle of wine.

The If You Don't Stop Whining
I May Start Screaming

Pour 7 ounces of soda water into a plastic cup with dishwasher stains. Add enough vodka to calm down. This pairs wonderfully with Handi-Snacks. You know, the "cheese" and cracker things. Don't bother with the plastic red triangle knife for spreading. In the comfort of your home feel free to just use your tongue to lick the spread out. Eat eight. Throw some cheese down to your toddler because you're a good parent.

OTHER FABULOUS PAIRINGS

Malt Liquor	Lays Potato Chips
White Wine	Warm Tater Tots or McDonalds Chicken Nuggets (sweet and sour sauce)
Guinness Beer	Slices of White Buttered Bread or Macaroni and Cheese
Budweiser	Memories from your old life

Gin	Anger
Bacardi	Whole milk
Shiraz	Goldfish crackers
Corona	Homemade nachos/your child's pizza crusts
Sangria	Dry store brand cereal and your tears
Pabst Blue Ribbon	Hot Pockets
Sparkling wine	Leftover pasta

If you're the cooking type, know that a drink in hand can take the sting out of having to prepare meals for your family. You may also need one while reading books like The Giving Tree during bedtime. If you're not familiar with The Giving Tree, it is a manual that teaches children how to be selfish little bastards.

The message here is simple: treat yo self.

> **Sanctiparent:** *"Wow. Alcohol is the answer for your inability to parent. You have a problem."*

> **Response:** *"Why the fuck are you still here?"*

CHAPTER 17
FATIGUE

The difference between babies and toddlers is that babies like to sleep. Most toddlers wake up at the butt crack of dawn. Combine that with the fact that they keep you at heightened state of awareness due to their assholery, and you've got a really tired parent on your hands.

There's no simple way to deal with the fatigue of having an Energizer Bunny in Osh Kosh running around your house. The first thing you can do to help yourself is to get a simple coffee machine. Find one like a Keurig or Tassimo that only requires you to push a button to get liquid energy. Espresso machines and machines that require you to put stuff in filters are way too much to deal with when you can barely remember what day it is.

Chances are that you won't actually remember to drink your coffee. You'll probably find it in the microwave at 5:30 when you're heating up Authentic Breaded Chicken Morsels for your kid.

It is essential that you find ways to lie down during the day. If you're at work, find a storage closet or curl up under your desk. If you have an office to yourself, let everyone know that you have a very important conference call scheduled and pass out on the floor.

Being the stay-at-home parent to a toddler presents challenges when finding time to doze. If your child naps, you'll probably want to spend the time they're unconscious putting away everything they've destroyed during the day and then treating yourself to some afternoon nachos.

Smart parents find ways to relax while their toddlers are awake. How do you do this? Simple. Make it a game.

Creating games that involve you lying down doing nothing is key to surviving long afternoons with a kid. Give these "activities" creative names that make it clear to your child that while you are physically present, you will not be moving and/or interacting.

Sample Game Names:

Sleeping Daddy

Hospital Invalid

Tiger With a Problem

Narcoleptic Friend

Sick Person With Eyes Closed

Broken Worm

I'm a Blanket

Quiet Mountain Mom

Dead Starfish

Play Around Me

Buy your toddler a $10 doctor's kit from a toy store and let them tap on your knees and stuff. Give them a washcloth, slotted spoon, and some lotion and just let them do random shit to you while you pretend to be somewhere else. Long toddler talons are fantastic for back scratching. Teach them to be useful. Close your eyes. You might fall asleep so be careful. If you should doze off, when you wake up your bag will be dumped out and your kid might be eating nail polish and tampon sandwiches.

NAPS

Toddlers must nap. They simply must. The time your toddler spends unconscious during the day will make the difference between you being sane and you losing your mind and running through the center of your town nude screaming prophecies.

If you can get your toddler to nap twice, great. If your toddler can only nap once, that's fine, too. Most people start their toddler's nap after lunch, say 1PM. A nice 1-3:30PM nap will change your life. You need the break. Don't try to get anything done lest the nap schedule look like this.

1PM – Get toddler to sleep.

1:15PM – Do dishes

1:35PM – Pick up family room

1:50PM – Wipe down surfaces

2PM – Start a load of laundry

2:10PM – Clean up bedroom

2:30PM – Attempt to figure out dinner. Throw some random stuff in crock pot

3PM – Feel good about everything you did and think, "Ahhh. Now to relax for a moment. I deserve it."

The second your ass touches the couch or your head hits your pillow, a sensor will go off in your child's psyche and he or she will immediately wake up crying.. Do you see what happened here? You tried to accomplish things and it came back to hurt you. Housework hurts. It hurts you bad. Never forget. Here's what you should have done:

1PM – Get toddler to sleep

1:05PM – TAKE OFF PANTS AND GET INTO BED

1:07PM – Netflix and food in bed

1:10PM – Fall asleep with a mouth full of shredded cheese

3PM – Hear toddler and get up. Put pants back on.

Is your house clean? No. But do you feel like listing your child on Craiglist? Also no.

Do the right thing. Fall asleep with food in your mouth with no pants. Cleaning during your downtime is for suckers and chumps.

The Witching Hour

Toddlers wake up from their naps like angry drunks; confused, belligerent, and somewhat emotionally abusive. We call the time period between the "wake up" and "finally asleep" period, The Witching Hour. Don't let the name confuse you, The Witching Hour does not last a mere 60 minutes. It lasts *the rest of the day*.

The Witching Hour is characterized by your child not allowing you to put them down and aggressive whining.

If you're the working parent to a stay-at-home spouse, this is why you need to rush home at the end of the day. Should you dawdle, you may find your toddler alone in a playpen with a bowl of crackers and a sippy cup of tap water alone. All that will remain of your spouse is a note on a table saying, "I told you to hurry. Bye."

It's normal for toddlers to cry between 3-4PM and their bedtime. Dinner prep will be next to impossible. Invest in a toddler carrier at some point and strap that kid to your back if you're truly committed to putting a meal together. Or don't and order take-out. Dinnertime will, as always, be hell as your child struggles with wave after wave of fatigue and having to eat something other than cereal.

The Witching Hour is when you're most likely to:

- Spend your family's life savings on Etsy
- Start drinking
- Indulge in a backyard cigarette
- File for divorce online
- Curse at your child

- Angry clean and throw out all of the markers
- Say you need to take out the trash and just linger in the alley next to your house for an hour
- Pretend to use the bathroom and play on your phone while sitting on the toilet
- Hide from your family in the garage behind boxes

BEDTIME

Putting a toddler to sleep is kind of like getting that one friend who has had too much to drink out of the bar and home. You're going to spend a lot of time talking softly but sternly to them about how they need to stop crying and just get in the cab. You might have to clean up their pee pee or vomit. You're going to listen to them talk about bullshit nonsense. They're going to need hugs. You're going to have to get them water. You might have to sit with them for awhile and listen to them get stupidly philosophical. They'll ask for more drinks and you'll have to tell them "NO." They'll request a meal. They'll tell you they love you and ask if you love them. They'll want to talk about every boo boo they've ever gotten. At the end of it all you'll be exhausted and make a mental note to next time withhold liquids from this person.

The difference between your encounter with your intoxicated friend who still hasn't learned that tequila should never be mixed with wine and the bedtime routine is that the latter will have to done on a *nightly basis*.

Despite knowing night comes like clockwork, toddlers seem surprised that bedtime keeps coming. They approach the event with sadness, rage, and some truly fucked up behavior. Many of them get diarrhea of the mouth and ask a series of essay questions designed to keep you their hostage. Others begin complaining about bug bites that healed months ago or blanket problems. Some just cry. Some are escape artists who take nightfall as an opportunity to reenact *The Shawshank Redemption*.

I have no advice for you other than to just press forward. Eventually your kid will pass out. You might also pass out in their little Elmo toddler bed.

To prepare yourself for the hell that is putting a toddler to bed, I've compiled a list of common toddler bedtime stalling techniques.

100 COMPLAINTS TODDLERS HAVE AT BEDTIME

1. My favorite toy is in the car.

2. My favorite toy is in the backyard.

3. My favorite toy is at the store and I don't own it yet. Can you buy it online?

4. My blanket is too hot.

5. My blanket is too cold.

6. My blanket is too scratchy.

7. My blanket smells like pee.

8. My pajamas are too big.

9. My pajamas are too small.

10. My pajamas are the wrong color.

11. The pajamas I need are in the washing machine.

12. I'm hungry.

13. I'm thirsty.

14. My hair hurts.

15. My finger hurts.

16. My toe hurts.

17. My mouth hurts.

18. My teeth hurt.

19. My butt hurts.

20. My eyelashes feel weird.

21. I feel sick.

22. Can you read me another story?

23. Can I have one more kiss?

24. Can I have one more hug?

25. Can you change the color of the moon?

26. What if Elmo is my real dad?

27. Who are you?

28. What are we doing tomorrow?

29. Are we poor?

30. What's your maiden name?

31. What's my social security number?

32. What country do we live in?

33. Am I adopted?

34. Are you adopted?

35. I want to live with grandma.

36. Why does your face look mad?

37. Why does your face look so old?

38. Why does your face have lines?

39. What happens when we die?

40. Can I take another bath?

41. Will you make me some popcorn?

42. How come your breath smells like beer?

43. Does Sid The Science Kid have ADHD?

44. What's your favorite color?

45. Do you want to build a snowman?

46. What's the opposite of hair?

47. Why is pee yellow?

48. Why is pee warm?

49. Can you get me different socks?

50. Can we change my pajamas again?

51. I'd like new sheets- can we change the sheets?

52. Can I have an orange?

53. Should I take my vitamins now?

54. How did I get here?

55. How are babies made?

56. Am I a robot?

57. Why do we need underwear?

58. Is poop made of chocolate?

59. Why is poop the same color as chocolate?

60. Do we have any chocolate?

61. Is tomorrow my birthday?

62. When is my birthday?

63. What am I getting for my birthday?

64. What color is my cake going to be?

65. Can you tickle my back?

66. Can you tickle faster/better?

67. How come you're falling asleep?

68. What is grass?

69. How many kinds of animals are there?

70. What are clouds made out of?

71. Have you ever been in a spaceship?

72. What is blood?

73. Can I watch TV?

74. Can I play on the iPad?

75. Can I go downstairs with you?

76. Can I sleep in your bed?

77. Can I have a sandwich?

78. Can I have some chocolate milk?

79. Is tomorrow Halloween?

80. Can I wear a Halloween costume right now?

81. Why are you crying?

82. Are you a goblin?

83. Am I royal?

84. What's 3 + 3?

85. Why?

86. Are you an Elsa or an Anna?

87. Can I fly?

88. Do I have any latent powers?

89. What is balloon?

90. Are you sleeping?

91. Can I just have a small snack?

92. Cheese?

93. Cracker?

94. Ok, an apple?

95. Can I finish my dinner now?

96. What's for breakfast?

97. What time is it?

98. Are you sleeping again?

99. Where are you going?

100. Can I have one more hug?

This is your life.

Sanctiparent: *"My child would never do this."*

Response: *"You're asking to get cut."*

CHAPTER 18
HOLIDAYS

Holidays help make up for the difficulty of having toddlers. They help you remember why you had children in the first place: the photo opportunities.

HALLOWEEN

On this magical night, you get to dress up your toddler like an idiot and parade them around town. It's your right. On Halloween, parents of toddlers have the opportunity to replenish their Night Stash for free.

Can toddlers trick or treat? Absolutely.

How To Use Your Kid To Get Free Candy

1. Teach your toddler to say "Twick o Tweet" in the cutest voice they can. Not "trick." TWICK. Switching the "r" for a "w" will

result in 20% more deliciousness for you to consume while watching The Late Show.

2. Invest in an adorable costume like a chicken, dog, or any kind of animal. Stay away from "ironic" costumes like band members, food, and dead people. Princesses are a dime a dozen and no longer stand out. The cuteness factor greatly affects how much candy your toddler will be given.

3. Leave the house at around 5:30PM. Any earlier than that and people will be hesitant to dig deep into their candy supply. They'll be in early-evening rationing mode.

4. Don't go to malls. Go door to door. If you live in squalor, drive to a nicer community. Look for well-maintained lawns, sculptures, butlers, and gold flakes floating through the air. If you can get into a gated community (try to piggy back on a car already rolling through) go for it. The full-sized Snickers bars will be worth it.

5. Bring a large 10-gallon bucket, baby bath, or heavy duty trash bag with you but keep it in the car. I'll explain this later.

6. Start trick-or-treating. Make sure your toddler says "Twick o Tweet" in a sweet voice and "Thank you." Stand behind them and

smile like you love your family. If your child has achieved maximum cuteness, you should get lots of candy.

7. When your candy bag is half full, go back to your car and dump it into your storage container or baby bath. Repeat until your child can no longer walk anymore. Allow your toddler 5-6 Skittles for energy to get through an additional 6-7 neighborhoods.

8. Within a few hours, you will have a large stash of candy in the trunk of your car courtesy of your little one. And you thought they weren't good for anything?

Additional Tips

Say things like, "Hurry honey, we have to go visit grandma at the rest home," loud enough for the candy holder to hear. Phrases like, "Last house, ok? I know you didn't get much candy but you have that blood transfusion in the morning" will also guarantee a bigger haul.

The day after Halloween is just as important as Halloween itself when it comes to replenishing your Night Stash. Don't go home- camp in your local big box store's parking lot. You want to be first in line to get those 75% off Halloween candy deals. This is our Narnia.

CHRISTMAS

Look, don't go all crazy getting your toddler—who doesn't even know their last name—expensive presents. You could wrap up items they already own and your kid would be delighted. Toddlers just like to unwrap shit. It reminds them of destroying. Wrap up plastic cups from your pantry, rawhide, spoons, a Ziplock bag of leaves, a quart of milk ...whatever you have. You don't need money to make Christmas special for your toddler. Toddlers do not care.

The best part of Christmas is using Santa to threaten them. If you're doing it right, Santa should sound like a cross between a sniper and the NSA: someone who is always watching them and ready to take serious, permanent action. Let them know that Santa will not let emotions get in the way of burning all of their gifts should they disobey. Get one of those creepy ass Elf on the Shelf things if you feel like it.

Don't get caught up in moving the Elf every night like it has a life of its own. That's demented.

BIRTHDAYS

No doubt you're going to want to throw a birthday party for your toddler despite the fact that most of them will spend the entire event crying. Keep it simple, but not so simple that people feel cheated out of their gifts. Hot dogs, fruit, vegetables, hamburgers, and a store bought cake are enough. Open a couple large bags of chips and dump them into a plastic bowl. Buy paper cups, plates, and disposable napkins. Throw candy at the kids. Quit with all this Pinterest shit. Remember, this is a birthday party, not a fucking wedding. Birthdays are a celebration of being that much closer to putting the toddler years behind you.

What To Buy a Toddler For Their Birthday

Congrats on being invited to a toddler's birthday party! I know you'd much rather spend your day sitting on a couch with no pants on with a glass of wine in hand, but if you don't go the parents will silently hate you for life. Don't forget to bring a pressie.

There are three categories of toddler gifts:

If you give a friend's toddler one of those "corn popper" devices that you push on the floor, the ones that sound like a drive-by shooting, consider yourself an enemy. Your parent friend will be just biding their time, waiting for you to have a kid of your own. One day when you least expect if they'll give your child something truly obnoxious like a set of kazoos or a caffeine lollipop. Don't play this game. Everybody loses.

Don't give paints unless you're also going to host the painting party in your home. For the love of everything holy do not give a toddler one of those play dough kits. Cleaning dried salt dough out of toy crevices, carpet, and floors is a bitch. Age inappropriate gifts like Rainbow Looms will burned.

If you don't have any money or common sense when it comes to presents, don't bring one. The kid probably has enough crap anyway.

CHAPTER 19
TANTRUMS

There is nothing fucking worse than your toddler falling to the ground in a crowded mall and throwing a tantrum. Tantrums can caused by a variety of reasons: hunger, fatigue, boredom, or just a desire to make you look like a jackass.

The best thing you can do when your kid starts to lose their shit in public is to get the hell out of wherever you are as fast as you can. Those threats under your breath aren't going to do jack when your toddler reaches that place of no return where their eyes roll back into their head. Only you know when your spawn has gone to the bad place wherein they won't be reasonable or respond to your voice. When that happens, get to your car as fast as you can. Knock over strangers if you have to.

Your toddler's biggest weapons during a tantrum aren't their gorilla yells or their crazy thrashing around: it's the audience. Toddlers are assholes but they're not idiots. They know that by embarrassing the fuck out of you they increase their chances of getting what they want. By going to your car, forcing them into their carseat, and taking them home, you've removed their source of power: your shame. Let them tantrum in the living room. Who cares? Toddler tantrums are a good opportunity for you to catch up on email until that little mofo calms down and is ready to act like a human again. It's not your job to sing "Swing Low Sweet Chariot" in your child's ear while they try to slap you in the face while screaming. Let them have their rage but let them also know that the world won't stop for them.

CHAPTER 20
POTTY TRAINING

Potty training is either a hellish experience or a piece of cake. There is no in-between. Toddlers either take to it like they were never in diapers or fight the potty like it is their sworn enemy. There is no way to know which kind of toddler you'll have. They decide amongst themselves months in advance. If you have an easy toddler, don't think it has anything to do with you. Anyone with more than one kid can tell you that you were just dealt a good hand so quit it with the high and mighty Facebook posts ya bitch.

You can buy all of the Pull Ups (expensive diapers), cloth training pants, sticker charts, M&Ms, and Skittles you want but what you really need to prepare for potty training is laundry detergent because you're gonna be washing. A lot. Make sure you have a bucket, mop, Clorox Wipes, and towels that you don't mind cleaning up butt nuggets and urine with.

Potty training a toddler turns you into a 24-hour janitor. I hope you like shaking wet turds out of a plastic potty into the toilet, because this will be your life for awhile.

Potty training means that you will visit every single public restroom in your city. You will experience the joy that is a urine soaked carseat. You will ponder skipping potty training all together and just settling into the idea that you will have a 4th grader in Huggies.

Don't rush potty training lest you become one of those parents who has to bear the shame of regression. Sure, tell everyone that your 18-month old is "fully trained." Just wait until that sucker turns two and you're buying Pull-Ups again. Those feelings of superiority will nose dive faster than a postpartum woman's sex drive.

Make potty training into a game. Not for the kid, for you.

The Toddlers Are Assholes Drinking Game

- Take a drink whenever your toddler takes a shit on the floor five seconds after you've pick them up from the potty where they were sitting for half an hour.

- Take a drink whenever your toddler screams that they urgently have to use the bathroom when you're in the grocery store line, airport security line, or the Department of Motor Vehicles line.

- Take a drink whenever your toddler needs to pee in a place with no bathroom forcing them to urinate between parked cars or behind a bush.

- Take a drink whenever your toddler convinces you that they need to use a public bathroom and then licks/touches/explores every disgusting surface despite your pleas.

- Take two drinks if your toddler pulls a used tampon out of the sanitary napkin metal disposal bin and asks, "Why is this kite bleeding?"

- Take a drink every time you pick up a hard turd with your bare hands.

- Take a drink every time your toddler pees on you, soaking you in their people juice down to your skin.

- Take two drinks for every ten loads of laundry you do.

- Take a drink every time your toddler pisses themselves in public and refuses to acknowledge it.

- Take a drink every time your toddler shits their pants and shakes the turd out of their pant leg casually.

- Take four drinks every time you think you're done with potty training when you're really not.

- Take a drink every time a "friend" tells you that their child was potty trained at 6-months old and then clock them in face for lying.

Life can be fun.

CHAPTER 21
ASSHOLE PARENTS

It wouldn't be fair to talk about the assholishness of toddlers without talking about their parental counterparts. Toddlers have an excuse when it comes to their shitty behavior: they're learning how to be people. If you're an asshole of a parent, it's all on you.

There are four main types of parents that we all hate. If you're one of these, know that we can't stand you. You might think you have friends, but you don't. You have an audience. We all talk shit behind your back and keep your around for entertainment and because our kids might be friends. Change your ways.

1. The Overly Competitive Parent

For shit's sake. Calm the fuck down about EVERY-THING. This parent believes that their child is an extension of their very fragile ego. Anything can be a sport with this asshole: whose kid is eating the healthiest, whose kid is going to the best school, whose kid is the funniest, whose kid is the cutest. You are a mess of a parent if you're making your child compete in the Parental Olympics 24/7.

If your Facebook page is all humblebrags, you might be an overly competitive asshole parent. If you are constantly one-upping, ("Oh your toddler is finally talking?" Mine just finished War & Peace"), you might be an overly competitive asshole parent. Newsflash: You do not have to respond to everything someone says about their kid with a fact about your own.

Overly competitive parent, why do you need so much applause? Did you not get enough attention as a child? Please, sort yourself out. You're exhausting.

2. Crazy Crunchy Parent

We get it. The world is full of toxins and we're all full of tumors and dying if we don't follow whatever special diet you're on this week. Vaccines are full of straight bleach, breastfeeding is the only way to go, formula is the devil's semen, regular school is for future dog rapists, plastic bottles will give your kids eye gonorrhea, and you have all of the answers. Thank you for the hourly Facebook links from obscure websites that back up your claims. We appreciate it. Thanks for picking apart our meals and lifestyles with your passive aggressive comments.

Look, we know you're not all wrong, but you make living a natural life look about as fun as joining a cult so we ignore you. PS. Shut the fuck up.

3. "I LOVE MY KIDS HEY GUYS DID I MENTION HOW MUCH I LOVE MY KIDS?" PARENT

This parent loves their kid so much that they can't stop telling everyone how much they love their kid just in case you forgot how much they love their kid. Hey douche, there are other ways to show your child how you feel for them without posting on social media that they aren't even on. Raving every now and then is fine, but if you go on and on about your genital fruit every damn day, you're annoying people. You might be one of these parents if you can't take your kid to the park without posting 6 million photos of them on the slide from different angles/outfits. Have you ever made a meal for your child that you haven't Instagramed? New parents with babies under two are given extra leeway, but don't push it.

These parents are like the Overly Attached Girlfriend meme and we suspect that just like her, what lies beneath is murderous rage.

4. Fake Perfect Parent

You are the scariest parent yet because when we look at the perfect images you post of your perfect family, we hear "NO WIRE HANGERS" echoing in our ears. If you can't share an image of your family online without editing it in Photoshop first, you fall into this category. It really is unnecessary to digitally whiten your 3 year-old's baby teeth. This parent is dedicated to sharing their crafts, balanced meals, and vacation photos so that everyone knows just how wonderful everything is in their life. If you're a slave to Pinterest fads and yell at your family to "smile at the camera," you might be a Fake Perfect Parent. If you write weekly Facebook status updates about how much you loOooOOve your husband, you might be a Fake Perfect Parent. Nobody loves their living spouse that much, sorry. If the photos you share never have an ounce of clutter, you might be a Fake Perfect Parent. We're not buying it though. This bigger the facade, the bigger whatever it is it's hiding.

CHAPTER 22
A FINAL WORD FROM THE MANAGEMENT

Parents have it hard these days. We might have more gadgets for raising kids, but we're more far more neurotic than the generations of moms and dads before us. Nowadays, we're all expected to make lunches in the shape of *Frozen* characters, put our kids in stylish clothes, spend our weekends making elaborate Pinterest balloon animal melted crayon ombre cookie crafts, and have our families and homes look like they just walked out of a page from Real Simple magazine— the pressure is enormous. And it's stupid. Fuck all that fake shit. No one is taking score. Raising kids is hard and raising toddlers feels IMPOSSIBLE most of the time. We all wonder if we're fucking it up, so why not just be honest? The kind of people parents need in their lives are the ones who they can call to come over and have a drink while their kids play on the floor while they bitch about their day. You should be able to say "Hey, toddlers are assholes," without them getting their panties in a wad. You should be able to say,

"I hate my fucking family sometimes" and "Cooking dinner sucks ass." Fuck all of this perfectionist, gratitude out the ass bullshit. It's ok to say it sucks when it sucks. Yes, there are people in the world who have it so much worse, but does that mean we can't let some steam off? Of course not.

You know what's harder than dealing with toddlers? Having to pretend it's not.

Want to chat? Find me on Facebook:

https://www.facebook.com/sophakingtyerd

I'm going to take a nap. Thanks for reading.

XO
Sopha King Tyerd